A Funny Way to Learn English

A Funny Way to Learn English

Eddie Boyle

Copyright © 2003 Eddie Boyle

Apart from any fair dealing for the purposes of research or private study, or criticism or review, as permitted under the Copyright, Designs and Patents Act 1988, this publication may only be reproduced, stored or transmitted, in any form or by any means, with the prior permission in writing of the publishers, or in the case of reprographic reproduction in accordance with the terms of licences issued by the Copyright Licensing Agency. Enquiries concerning reproduction outside those terms should be sent to the publishers.

Published by
Matador
12 Manor Walk, Coventry Road
Market Harborough
Leics LE16 9BP, UK
Tel: (+44) 1858 468828 / 469898
Email: books@troubador.co.uk
Web: www.troubador.co.uk/matador

The author may be contacted at etboyle@blueyonder.co.uk

ISBN 1 899293 48 5

Cover: © Corbis

The publisher makes no representation, express or implied, with regard to the accuracy of the information contained in this book and cannot accept any legal responsibility or liability for any errors or omissions that may be made.

Typesetting: Troubador Publishing Ltd, Market Harborough, UK
Printed and bound in the United Kingdom by Henry Ling Limited, at the Dorset Press, Dorchester, DT1 1HD

Matador is an imprint of Troubador Publishing Ltd

Contents

Introduction vii

LESSONS 1–18

ONE	Punctuation	3
TWO	The Apostrophe	8
THREE	It's and Its	12
FOUR	Redundancy	15
FIVE	Abused Words	19
SIX	Ambiguity	22
SEVEN	A Wee Bit of Grammar	26
EIGHT	Some Parts of Speech	31
NINE	Some More Grammar	37
TEN	The Inelegant Sentence	41
ELEVEN	Metaphors and All That	44
TWELVE	Sentence Joining	48
THIRTEEN	More About the Sentence	54
FOURTEEN	Tense	62
FIFTEEN	Through the Alphabet	66
SIXTEEN	Spelling	84
SEVENTEEN	Words that Work	86
EIGHTEEN	For Amusement Only	89

ANSWERS 93

TO
MY FAMILY
CHILDREN
GRANDCHILDREN
GREAT-GRANDCHILDREN

Introduction

A Funny Way To Learn English is not a grammar book – it is a book about grammar, which aims to teach you the basic points of the English language in a humorous and enjoyable way. This is not intended to be a comprehensive guide to all aspects of English grammar – there are many other books which do that, and you'll find they're all far larger than this one! What I intend to do here is teach most of the basics of English grammar by example – usually with examples of incorrect language usage that are, I hope, amusing.

As a teacher for 40 years in Scottish primary, junior secondary, comprehensive schools, and 18 years teaching English in night school, I can not but help noting that the corrections I made in English at the start of my career are the same as when I retired. These occur, not only in the classroom, but also in the newspapers, radio, TV and even in Parliament.

If you feel that your English is a bit shaky and are not sure when to use *I* or *me*, *its* or *it's*, *sang* or *sung*, *who* or *whom* and can't tell a pronoun from a preposition, then this is the wee book for you. This book deals with simple, basic grammar, and not too much of that, the commonest spelling errors, sentence construction, punctuation and vocabulary, all that is needed to acquire passable English. Be comforted by the fact that many of my collection of howlers (amusing examples of English misuse) come from Prince Philip, Elton John and others among the elite.

Test yourself in the 20 sentences on pages ix and x, and if you get 15 right then you needn't buy this book – unless you want to give your granny a present. Come to think of it, your granny probably knows more about grammar than you...!

Some of the test sentences have no mistakes, others will have one or perhaps two. The answers are briefly given on pages 95 and 96, and are more fully explained as you read through the book.

One tip before you start any study. Buy a dictionary and a thesaurus. It is amazing what you can find in a dictionary. Page 318 of my 1979 edition deals with History (Congress of Vienna), literature (Congreve), botany (conifers), geography (Coniston Water), grammar (conjugate and conjunction), medicine (conjunctivitis) and magic (conjuration). The dictionary also provides help in pronunciation, derivation of words, defines all the parts of speech with examples, figures of speech with examples, like "burning your boats," "grass widow," American spelling and tables of weights and measures. You can buy a paperback thesaurus nowadays for £1.

Test Your Knowledge!

1. The BHB (British Horseracing Board) went on the attack yesterday. It's leaders are to ask the Government to repeat a turnover-based levy scheme for 2002–03. (Source: *Daily Mail*, 9th November 2001.)
2. During the course of the night, the wind and rain will spread across the whole of the British Isles with the exception of areas in the south of England.
3. From a bye kick and with wind assistance, the Aberdeen goalie scored from his own penalty area against Raith Rovers, surely the most unique goal ever.
4. *Scenes of Crimes*. 8pm, Thursday 8th November 2001 "How the police trailed the killer of a shopkeeper who left bloody footsteps while getting away". (Source: *Daily Mail TV magazine*.)
5. To make sure of your Sunbeam toaster guarantee, please complete the enclosed form within 10 days and return to the given address.
6. Can I come with you as one of your crew on you're maiden voyage down the Clyde to Sliddery?
7. Although the fully laden holiday plane skidded off the runway into a nearby lake, none of the 320 passengers was injured.
8. After a great deal of controversy, the once famous steel complex at Ravenscraig was razed in view of hundreds of former workers.
9. It was through the instrumentality of Samuel Plimsoll and his Plimsoll Line that his idea saved the lives of countless seamen.
10. Elton John says he is literally petrified at the thought of making his first appearance at the

Edinburgh Festival.
11. "Are you doing anything tomorrow night?"
"No."
"I'm not doing nothing either." (Source: *Coronation Street.*)
12. Louis Theroux, all six foot two of him, stretched out on one of Jimmy Saville's luxuriant white leather couches. (Source: *Sunday Herald.*)
13. When you look into a person's eyes, you sometimes wonder what's going on in their head, especially if it is Richard Branson. (Source: *Sunday Herald*, 2001.)
14. Mrs Thatcher was reported to have said that she was pleased with the final outcome of the conference.
15. If you stop smoking you will soon save enough money to buy a TV or go on holiday to Torquay, etc, etc.
16. The two neighbouring councils agreed in principal that in future their schools would not have seperate times for the Autumn holiday.
17. The parachutist landed safely in the hay field and there were men working in it and they ran to help him.
18. It is strange the Conservatives have not privatised British Rail considering the vast amount of money being poured into its seemingly bottomless tunnels.
19. The Prime Minister was warned that if nothing was done, the trouble in Kosovo would escalate further.
20. General Custer carefully studied the maps of the surrounding territory. He immediately ordered the attack on the Indians.
    Join these two sentences in three ways:
    (a) by a conjunction,
    (b) by a relative pronoun,
    (c) by a participle phrase.

LESSONS 1-18

The Druids were happy under the Mistletoe and that's how kissing under it started

Lesson One

Punctuation

A wee story, a true one, to show the importance of punctuation.

Some years ago, British Rail was closing down scores of stations, one of them, Drem, near Edinburgh. The instructions were to "retain Drem station bridge." The demolishers took this to mean that they had to move everything but the bridge. The man carting off the last of the debris had his doubts, and suggested to the gaffer, "What if there has been a mistake in the demolition order?"

Indeed, there had been a mistake. BR had made a list of all facilities it wanted to keep, but in the case of Drem station it stated, "Drem station bridge to be retained." The demolishers thought that meant only the bridge was to be preserved, inferring everything else was to be demolished. The instruction should have read, "Drem station, bridge to be retained." An expensive missing comma as everything had to be replaced. There was no need for a comma, and BR could have saved heavy expense by using the conjunction 'and' – "Drem station *and* bridge to be retained."

Let's look at some punctuation we have already used on pages i and ii. The first sentence, a fairly long one, ends as all sentences must, with a full stop at 'way'.

The second, *"These occur, not only in the classroom, but also in the newspapers, radio, TV and even in Parliament."* has a list of four items and it is usual to put a comma between each, with the word 'and' between the last two.

Commas

Commas may change the meaning of a sentence. There's a big difference between:

> Nanki Poo thinks wee Hughey is wrong.
> Nanki Poo, thinks wee Hughey, is wrong.
> Pardon impossible, to be sent to Siberia.
> Pardon, impossible to be sent to Siberia.

Try making sense of: *That that is is that that is not is not is not that it it is.*

When punctuated this becomes: *That that is, is. That that is not, is not. Is not that it? It is.*

In other words, *That that exists, exists. That that does not exist, does not exist. Is not that so? It is.*

Exclamation Marks

Exclamation marks are for exclamations, *Oh! Jings!* as its name suggests, for commands, *Halt! Hurry!* and for warnings, *Danger! Foot and Mouth Disease.*

Quotation Marks

Quotation marks must give the exact words of a speaker, no more, no fewer.

For example, the reporter may have chosen not to use Mrs Thatcher's words in sentence 14 on page x, and not

---

Druids were the ones the romans torchered for kissing under mistletoe.

quoted her word for word. She may have correctly said, *"I am pleased with the outcome of the conference,"* but the reporter added the word *'final'*.

Direct Speech

Direct speech involves quotation marks, as in *Mrs Thatcher said, "I am pleased with the outcome of the conference."*

Note the use of a capital letter to start, and a comma before the quotation marks are opened. At the end there is a full stop, then the closing quotation marks.

The quotation may be broken for variety. *"I am happy," said Mrs Thatcher, "with the outcome of the conference."*

Note that there is a comma at the end of the first part, after 'happy', and to start the second part a small letter is used, for this is the second part of the same sentence.

You may, of course hear direct speech On Auchenshuggle TV. Last night, Stu McCookin, celebrity cook, advised, *"Rhubarb is good for you but only the stalk. Never eat the leaves."* You could write to the programme director in indirect speech, Stu McCookin tells us not to eat rhubarb leaves. Sure that's ancient. My mother told me that years ago.

Watch for the quote within a quote. In the US Senate, some years ago, a Democrat addressed the Republican President thus, *"In a broadcast to the nation, you said, 'Watch my lips. There will be no increase in taxation.' Then later, you do exactly that."* The inside quote is in single quote marks

Be careful if the inside quote comes at the end. *"Years*

Brochs were big towers you ran to hide in war for they had so high doors nobody could not get in.

ago, our Careers master advised us, 'Always take care of the molehills and the mountains will take care of themselves.'" We use the usual marks for direct speech, then the start of the inner quote at 'always' and the final two lots at the end.

Exercise 1.1
Your first homework

Turn the sentences below into (a) direct speech, then (b) indirect speech, using punctuation correctly. An example is given first.

Example
where are you going to my pretty maid asked the farmer.

(a) "Where are you going to, my pretty maid?" asked the farmer. (Direct speech.)
(b) The farmer asked the pretty maid where she was going to. (Indirect speech.)

1. will you walk into my parlour said the spider to the fly.
2. stop the bus yelled Margie ive left my handbag
3. it is easier to learn bulgarian than I thought claimed the young greek girl
4. boil my eggs for three minutes only insisted aunt emma i like to dip my toast in soft yolk
5. if you are not up yet andy mother shouted you will be too late for your train be down in a minute

The Romans built a wall between the Clyde and the Tyde.

Lesson One - Punctuation

for my cornflakes he shouted back

6. what can i get you for christmas my darling clementine one of those donut machines duncan so I can make lips-smacking donuts in my very own kitchen.

7. ladies and gentlemen announced miss stirrat let me introduce our speaker for this evening she is none other than the first woman to cross the firth of clyde in a bath tub from brodick to saltcoats miss le farge ladies and gentlemen

8. my great uncle Tobias asked me what had happened to ethan frome and ottokar kraus and I had to tell him id never heard of them but I would do my best to find out.

9. why do tv adverts my pal geordie asked not give you the chance to jot down phone and email numbers its as bad as the traffic lights that give you six and a half seconds not nearly enough time

Answers can be found on page 97

Doomsday Book was a prayer book that came out in the time of the Romans but Julius Caesar did not agree with it.

Lesson Two

The Apostrophe

When I started collecting howlers, I soon amassed so many on the apostrophe, I stopped because they had lost their rarity value. However with the coming of subtitles on TV I had to start again, and they are still occurring. There are two uses of the apostrophe: first to show possession; and secondly, to denote that a letter or letters are omitted.

Possession

The Possessive rule is simple, add the apostrophe and s.

Girl girl's   boy boy's   man man's   men men's
    woman woman's   women women's

The girl's toy was broken, the girl's toys were broken, the children's toys were broken.

Girl's stays the same whether she has a toy, singular, or toys, plural. Men, women and nouns like them, seamen, policewomen, add the apostrophe and the s. *You can never have mens', womens', childrens', no matter if singular or plural follows.*

For example, on Sunday, June 23, BBC 2 announced at the end of the European Athletic Championship, "The

Lesson Two - The Apostrophe

British mens' athletic team win the championship." Tut tut, BBC 2.

> The woman's purse was stolen in the market.
> The women's cloakroom is now open.
> The women's purses were stolen by Santa in his grotto.
> The women's keys were found.

Now for the tricky bit. *For words ending in S, put the apostrophe after the S.* The plural of most words end in S: girls, boys, sailors, players, doctors, fools and horses. So we have the girls' playground, the boys' yard, the sailors' hornpipe, the doctors' surgery,

Try to see the sense of the possessive. You cannot have *the girl's playground* or *the boy's yard*, for there is no such thing as a playground for one girl (*the girl's playground*) nor a yard for one boy (*the boy's yard*). Nor would a trade union be for one person only, as a Sunday newspaper had it, "Mr Higgins, Secretary of the Player's Union", but several doctors could share a surgery at the health centre, "Our doctors' surgery is always busy."

Confusion arises when the plural is not made by adding S but in some other way. For example,

> Lady, ladies   child, children
> man, men   mouse, mice.

This advert appeared in the press, "Ladie's coat for sale, real fur. £250." There is no such word as ladie, so it cannot be expressed thus. It should be 'lady's. Another advert was for a ladies' fur coat, which would mean that the one coat was shared by more than one person.

Columbus set out to discover America but only got as far as Iona.

The advert *"Cheapest fishermens' waders at Grantham's"* should be fishermen's, like men's. However, the apostrophe at Grantham's is correct because the word 'shop' or 'emporium' is not written or said but is 'understood'.

It is commonly accepted that apostrophes may be used for other living creatures and for some inanimate objects. Pet owners refer to the dog's collar, the cat's brush, the canary's water dish. It is no surprise that proud car and boat owners claim, "She's a beauty."

However, we would have to talk about cutting the edge of the lawn rather than the lawn's edge, and tidying the top of the wardrobe rather than the wardrobe's top.

Be wary of possessive adjectives like 'mine', 'ours', 'yours', 'hers' and 'theirs', which never take an apostrophe. "You do your thing and I'll do mine." Never mine's.

Names ending in S may cause difficulty. It is really a personal choice for some of them because there is no set rule to determine what is right in English. For example, compare the pronunciation of Moses and Burns. With a double S, Moses has a hissing sound and Burns more of a Z sound. It does not sound right to give them an apostrophe S, as in "Moses's brother was called Aaron", or "A Burns's Supper features the haggis". It is better to omit the S altogether.:

Moses' brother
A Burns' Supper

However, it is harder to decide in the cases of Thomas and James, for both ways sound OK.

Columbus discovered the United States of America but not on purpose.

St Thomas' School Wishaw,
St Thomas's School Wishaw.

St James' Park, Newcastle.
St James's Park Newcastle.

On balance, I would have St Thomas' and St James's, but this one is down to personal preference!

Exercise 2.1
Which of these is impossible?

My aunt's house
My aunts' house
My aunt's houses
My aunts' houses

William Wallace was cut to ribbons and a bit put up in every part of Scotland.

Lesson Three

It's and Its

The confusion between these two words, especially on TV and in the newspapers, makes it the most common mistake in my collection, so it deserves special mention. *Its* is a word in its own right, just like *yours, hers, computer* or *keyboard*:

- Our dog, Juppy, is daft for it is always chasing its own tail.
- Despite the mountainous waves, the tiny trawler ploughed its way safely to port.

As for the other *it's*, it's entirely different, for it is a combination word, in that it is short for *it is*.

We Brits love to take short cuts, whether across a busy railway line or a muddy field. This is also done with words, so instead of television we say TV, and we now have 'pram' for perambulator, and 'bus 'for omnibus. The second use for the apostrophe in *it's* is to show where we make the short cuts:

- It's stands for it is. The apostrophe is put in for the missing I.
- Don't means do not, and you see plainly that the 'o' is replaced by the apostrophe.

Common short cuts are, can't, didn't, doesn't, couldn't, shouldn't and won't. Therefore you use *it's* when you take

Lesson Three - It's and Its

the short cut for *it is*. Take the case above of Juppy never catching it's tail. It would be silly to read that he could not catch it is own tail!

My milk carton stated last week, "Our milk in a class of it's own". It was meant to be a clever play on the 'glass' that I would drink my milk from, but to me it read, "In a class of it is own".

Notice that apostrophes are also needed in other short cuts:

- The game starts in an hour's time.
- Two weeks' holiday isn't much.
- The rain's started.

Sometimes the plural ending in *s* is confusing – you often see mistakes made in shops:

- Canary banana's at their best.
- Two packs of onions' for the price of one.
- Todays' bargains! Coffee down 50 pence. Potatoes' too!
- Our sales' start on Friday.

No apostrophe is needed for bananas, onions, potatoes or sales. Whoever wrote the 'bargains' poster was probably misled by the plural 'bargains', and put the apostrophe after the 's'. It should have been, as you no doubt noticed, "Today's bargains".

Ikea opened it's second store in Scotland today with a

During the Black Death carts went out shouting bring out your dead bring out your dead!

surprise for one of it's customers. (From *STV news*.)

No doubt its Swedish owners would be surprised that a Scottish television company does not know how to use the apostrophe!

Exercise 3.1
Make any necessary corrections

1. It's a pity the games had to be cancelled because of the frost.
2. The clinic's too far away for some of the older citizen's.
3. The whole school was on tenterhooks waiting the inspectors report.
4. Co-Op advert: Childrens' pyjamas, £3.99. Children's tights, £1.25. Childrens coats, £11.
5. When Winters' at its worst, Antartex coats are best.
6. John Knox's sermons in 1559 caused rioting and mobs stripping alter's.
7. Tottenham Hotspur's goalkeeper's a Scottish internationalist.
8. Colonel Stinko's trying to take over the worlds' supply of fresh air.
9. I ve left my good umbrella in the ladys' cloakroom.
10. Far too many seamen's lives were lost in the old days when ships were overloaded.

The Roundheads were the ones that shaved their hair to get their heads to fit their helmets.

Lesson Four

Redundancy

This is the most common howler after the apostrophe. Redundancy is the use of unnecessary words, or *verbosity, tautology, pleonasm*, whatever you like to call it. We shall see examples in this lesson. All these definitions basically mean the same, using too many words, and there's no need to learn the names in italics unless you want to. Let's look at some examples.

The second sentence on page ii is a good example, and most weather forecasters must have it in their manuals. Sentence 8 is also common as most people add *to the ground*. Sentence 12 is verbose, using *personally present* and *myself*. Read the sentence without these words and it still makes sense. More examples.

- "I knew both his wife and himself and got on well with both of them."

There are only two in the relationship, so *both* may be left out.

Some examples are so obvious that you wonder why the TV editors didn't catch on, as we can see from the following:

- "Every year car workers at Longbridge have an annual pay review." *Every year and annual?*
- "The new fire regulations are both necessary and essential." Here, *both* should be dropped and

either *necessary* or *essential*. Or perhaps add *absolutely* before *necessary*.
- "We are making progress in the right direction." Football coach interviewed after his team drew 1–1 at home following five successive defeats.

Mistakes often occur in words that start with RE: 're' *indicates a return to a previous condition. Return* is itself an example. You would return from your holiday, not return back:

- "It is to be hoped that the riot scenes at the Hagler v Minter fight will never recur again". **Recur** *means to occur again, so* **again** *is redundant. (An example from the BBC!)*
- "We will resume again," said the chairman, "at half past eight, after the coffee break". *Again,* **again** *is redundant here.*
- PC Dibble asks Top Cat, "Would you repeat that again?" *Either the PC made this mistake of repetition or he was asking TC for the third time.*
- "We must intervene in Kosovo before things escalate further". *Escalate means to increase in extent or intensity, so* **further** *is not needed.*
- "If we are to avoid this kind of thing (overcrowding at football matches) we must look forward to the future". *If you look to the future it can be only forward, so* **forward** *is unnecessary.*

The third kind of redundancy is like *raze*, where that word is sufficient in itself:

Nelson was a famous sailor who said of his medals 'I won them in war and I will die with them on in war just before he died.

Lesson Four - Redundancy

- "You don't know about the Darien Scheme? It's time then you were learning something about the past history of Scotland". *All history must be of the past by definition.*
- "Events like these that have happened in North Lanarkshire should be investigated by the Secretary of State for Scotland". *Events have to happen but you don't have to say so.*
- "Billy and I would like to revisit Chatanooga again". *OK, Billy but this will be at least your third visit.*

Exercise 4.1
Try these for yourself

1. Mr. Nicholas Winterton said that Mr. Pryor, the Secretary of State for Northern Ireland, should be sacked for crass ineptitude and blatant incompetence.
2. Research has shown that first born children are less popular at school than their younger brothers and sisters who are born after them.
3. The trouble of positioning of a job centre in the centre of Dumfries is that it would be terribly visually obvious.
4. "There is no way we are going to allow crazy lunatics to spoil our glorious game of football.
5. As we expected, having heard him before, Mr

Abraham Lincoln said at Gettysburg – Father forgive them for they know nor whar they do.

Chapman began his speech with a very good beginning.
6. When things are not going well as at West Ham at the moment, everything seems to go against you.
7. If we go back to the Middle Ages, hundreds of years ago, music did not play any part in the lives of ordinary people.
8. The original prototype of the first computer was a huge thing of several tons in weight.
9. It may not look if the snow will come to the Highlands for skiing but there is still hope yet.
10. When he got to Downing Street, the Chancellor avowed that his first priority would be to lower the rate of inflation.

The men and women of Paris threw bricks at the Bastille to show the toffs they werent feart for them.

Lesson Five

Abused Words

Sentence 3 (p ix) describes the goal scored by the Aberdeen goalie as *unique*, but it wasn't. Many such goals have been scored, so it is not unique – unique means the only one in the world. Neither can it be qualified as *most*, *more* or *very*. There are many other such abused words.

Sentence 10 (page x) tells us that Elton John is *literally* petrified at the thought of the Edinburgh Festival, but he cannot be, for literally stands for "*the exact meaning of the word*", and the exact meaning of petrified is 'turned into stone'. Elton might have felt as if he were being turned into stone at the thought, but he is still alive and performing. He could have used a figure of speech. *"I am petrified at the thought of appearing in Edinburgh."*

A boss once described Ravenscraig steelwork in Motherwell as *"literally bleeding to death."* because of a strike. A steelwork bleeding!

'Perfect'

Perfect is the most abused word of all. If someone or something is perfect, there is no way it can be bettered; it is complete, excellent, faultless.

- "At the show, the Aberdeen Angus was the most perfect example of beef on the hoof."

Leave out 'most' and the sentence will be perfect!

- "The American Founding Fathers were optimists in hoping for a more perfect Union."

If something is perfect, how can it become 'more' perfect?

'Inaccessible'

Inaccessible means you cannot get to it for some reason or other, so how did the police find a lost boy in the most inaccessible part of the moor? They couldn't have found him in an inaccessible part of the moor, let alone in the most inaccessible part. There were also the intrepid climbers tackling three peaks in a remote and inaccessible part of Chile. Like 'perfect', there are no 'more or most inaccessible' places, although there could be more or most accessible places in Chile.

'Universal'

> With 135 countries competing, these Olympic Games will be the most universal ever.

If the Games were universal, every country would be competing. "A record number of 135 countries will be competing in the Olympic Games." would be better.

'Awful'

A teacher of English advised our class to use the word

General Montgomery scoured the 7 seas to find the rock where his father fought the japs.

'awful' only to describe something catastrophic, like the Day of Judgement. Today, he would probably add the dropping of an atomic bomb. It is used in so many ways as to weaken it:

- "It was an awful (or awfully) good holiday, picnic, film, day, night, wedding, fish supper.
- A newspaper reports, "An awful lot of new restaurants are opening in Brussels for the increasing number of Eurocrats."

It meant a great many new restaurants were opening, not necessarily awful ones.

'Actual'

Well, maybe not abused, perhaps over used. I cannot actually recall an actual sentence that did not actually read the same without your actual *actually*.

'Poised'

A word that always conjured up for me a graceful diver, balanced on her toes on the high dale and plunging splashless, into an Olympic pool. Now journalists have 'got at it'.

- "OAPs over 75 poised to get free TV licence." I'm one and I haven't poised anywhere.
- "Australia poised to take the Ashes back home".

Joan went into the ark to get out of the rain of terror.

Lesson Six

Ambiguity

A sentence which is carelessly worded and may have two meanings:

> Edinburgh pours more sewage into the Forth than any other place.

This is an ambiguous statement. It should read, either Edinburgh pours more sewage into the Forth than any other town does, or Edinburgh pours more sewage into the Forth than it does into any other location. After all, filth is dumped into lochs, ponds and burns. Presumably in this case, the Forth gets the filth.

> "It appears that women find it harder to give up smoking than men."

Which is it? Do they find it harder to give up smoking than they do to give up men? We can assume they can not stop smoking as easily as men do, but we should not have to make assumptions.

> "Sevy Ballesteros hopes to use the clubs he helped to design in the Philippines next week."

This is not so ambiguous as the above for we realise Sevy is not using the clubs he designed next week, but that he is playing next week. All would have been well if 'next week'

Lesson Six - Ambiguity

came at the beginning of the sentence.

Sentence 5 (page ii) showed carelessness in Sunbeam Electrics. You were meant to complete the form and post it within the ten days, but following the wording, you could keep the toaster for weeks before sending them the form.

Which would you buy for dinner? Smoked Scottish salmon or Scottish smoked salmon? Smoked Scottish salmon for sure, because it is fish caught in Scottish waters and smoked, maybe in Scotland or elsewhere. Scottish smoked salmon is salmon that could come from Norway but which is smoked in Scotland.

> "A 200-channel service from Sky will start on Thursday, bringing with it the prospect of pay per-view of Premiership football matches and movies starting every 15 minutes." (Source: *Daily Mail*, September 1998.)

Sky can send out video movies every 15 minutes but not live football matches, so 'and of Premiership football matches' should come after '15 minutes.'

Sometimes the ambiguity is just daft:

> "Sir Julian Hodge, the Cardiff banker, has been notified that before his death the Pope created him a Knight of St. Gregory the Great."

It would be simpler if it was written as, "Before he died, the Pope created....."

Laws, rules, regulations and announcements have to be carefully worded so clever lawyers and clever members of

---

Napoleon died on an island surrounded by water.

the public do not manipulate. For instance, Safeway had a notice at the checkout that read, "Safeway magazines free only to those with an ABC card." I had such a card but not in my possession that day and was about to be charged 75 pence, so hastily put it back. Being in a hurry, I did not call the manager and argue that I did have a card but as the notice did not specify, as it should have, that I had to show it, I was entitled to the magazine.

A notice in a Florence hotel stated, "when guests occupy a three bed room, one guest will be entitled to a free breakfast." My wife and I were in such a room, but I did not feel like putting the point to the manager, who spoke fractured English.

I once asked a pupil, "What do the natives of the monsoon areas of Asia normally grow?" He answered, "Wet." I learned from then on to frame my questions more carefully.

Exercise 6.1
For you to decipher

1. The Beverley Sisters confused everyone yesterday by turning up in the same lemon outfits for the wedding of sister Teddy at London's Caxton Hall. The only give-away was the £40,000 emerald cut solitaire ring on Teddy's wedding finger which once belonged to Elizabeth Taylor. (Source: *Daily Express.*) Count your fingers, Liz!

One of the men that united Italy was Garry Baldy.

Lesson Six - Ambiguity

2. For the first time in their history Christie's are selling a shrunken head. It is included in a sale of tribal art on April 27th. Reserve price for the revolting article – catalogued as "Fine Jivaro" and about the size of an orange – £150. The owner, perhaps understandably, wishes to remain anonymous. (Source: William Hickey column, *Daily Express*.)
3. The will of an Irish shirt maker was found in the pocket of a pair of trousers he had sent to the cleaners three years after he died. (Source: *Daily Express*.)
4. They were frightened when the candle blew out and shouted for help.
5. Drunk fined £2,000 for assault on plane.
6. Councillors hold conference on town esplanade.
7. Recently retired from the Royal Engineers, Fred A Lang has written his first poem on a German helmet.
8. You don't find players like Michael Owen standing at street corners.
9. Fallen junk bond king, Michael Milken, one of Wall Street's most influential figures, is serving a ten year sentence for fraud at a US government work camp near San Francisco.
10. Barrow fined for illegal payments.

It is called the lyre bird for it tries to kid the people where its nest is not.

Lesson Seven

A Wee Bit of Grammar

Sentence 7 on page ix:

> Although the full laden holiday plane skidded off the runway into a nearby lake, none of the 320 passengers was injured.

It looks wacky, *'none of the 320 passengers was injured,'* but it is correct for the subject of the sentence is *none*, which is a pronoun meaning *not one*. The sentence therefore could read, *'not one of the 320 passengers was injured'*. It is made up of two parts, called CLAUSES; the first part, *'Although the fully laden holiday plane skidded off the runway'*, is a SUBORDINATE clause, for you feel it does not make sense on its own, you want to know what happened to the plane and its passengers. The second phrase, *'none of the 320 passengers was injured'*, is the INDEPENDENT or PRINCIPAL clause, for it makes sense on its own. The subject of the whole sentence is 'none', which is singular and must take a singular verb 'was'. This is a rule that we must always observe, and is the reason we have *I am* and not *I are,* and *she is* and not *she am*.

Every sentence must have a subject – the person or thing we are talking about – and a predicate, that is what we say about the subject. The subject will be a noun or a pronoun, and the predicate will be a verb:

'Dogs bark'. *Subject* dog. *Predicate* barks.

Some sentences may have an object. *Dogs bark at postmen.* Postmen is in the object at which the dogs bark and is said to be objective after the PREPOSITION *at*.

Preposition

Prepositions come before a noun or a pronoun and are important, for they show the relationship of that noun or pronoun to some other word in the sentence. Common prepositions are *to, by, in, into, for, from, with, without, through, over, under, above, below, beside, past.*

I put my biro *on, beside, beneath, under, over, by, with,* my diary.

A preposition can make a big difference to the sense of a sentence, as in:

The cashier took £3483 to the bank
A bandit took £3483 from the bank.

If we use a pronoun in place of the noun *postmen*, we must use the objective pronoun *them*. 'Dogs bark at them'.

- *The subject is always a noun or a pronoun, one word or more than one word.*
- *The predicate is always a verb, one word or more.*
- *The object is always a noun or a pronoun, one or more than one word.*

SUBJECT	PREDICATE	OBJECT
At the age of 59, Desperate Dan	still loves	hot cowpie with chips

Pronoun

A *pronoun* is often used in place of a *noun,* for it would be monotonous to use Desperate Dan all through a story. *He, him* and *himself* are the pronouns used for Dan and other males.

She, her and *herself* are for Miss Piggy, and *they, them,* and *you* for both males and females in the plural. *It* is used for non humans.

At the end or middle of a sentence it's sometimes difficult to decide – *he* or *him, I* or *me, we* or *us, she* or *her, we* or *us*? A clue can be found on page 12, where I mentioned our love of shortcuts. Let's take a look at a 'mistake' made by the Duke of Edinburgh addressing a throng of listeners:

"I thank you all for the warmth of your welcome to the Queen and I."

He was taking a shortcut instead of going the whole way round.

I thank you all for the warmth of your welcome to the

This is not the hoover that invented the cleaner, this one was only president of America.

Lesson Seven - A Wee Bit of Grammar

Queen and I also thank you for the warmth of your welcome to...... *I* or *me*?

You know it's *me*, and if the queen hadn't been there, he would have said *me*.

> "Me and Jim have a holiday planned when he gets out of the jail."

That was Liz in 'Coronation Street' and a bit of premature planning as Jim is still in clink. But let her say it without the shortcut.

> "Me has planned a holiday when Jim gets out of jail and Jim has planned a holiday when he gets out of jail."

Me has planned a holiday! No, not even Liz would make that mistake if she were on her own.

Here are the pronouns used as the subject and as the object:

SUBJECT: I, You, He, She, We, They, It,

OBJECT: Me, Us, You, Him, Her, Them , It.

The main occupation of the people of Norway is slumbering.

Exercise 7.1
Correct the following

Some of these sentences are correct, others are not.

1. It was the smartest decision made by John Lawrence when he decided to build a home for himself, you and I, 60 years back.
2. Tam got better marks in his English but he's a bit older than I.
3. Swimming is just as important for racehorses as for we human beings.
4. Official figures show that the amount of beer and whisky being consumed in Scotland in the last 18 months have plummeted – due to unemployment and the recess.
5. Ian Wright is one of a number of footballers who are leaving the field to take their talents into show business.
6. It is only a combination of these measures, spectator segregation, seating and a ban on alcohol, that is successful in keeping order at football matches.
7. Us old married can give young ones a tip or two on the art of living it up.

Last night in the terrible storm hundreds of chime chimb lums were blown down in our village.

Lesson Eight

Some Parts of Speech

Sentence 4 (p. ii). As we have already seen, *them* is a pronoun and cannot be used as an adjective to describe *posters*. The required adjective here is *those*, which is a *pointing out* (or demonstrative) adjective along with *this*, *that* and *these*.

You do not need to remember *demonstrative* or the names of diverse parts of speech, for many words may be different parts of speech: nouns, adjectives, verbs, adverbs and prepositions. Take the word *round*, for example.

- Tiger Woods could do a round of golf at Saint Andrews in 62 and I would take 102 if I were in my best form. **NOUN** because it is the NAME of something.
- In Scotland you can buy round or square sausage. **ADJECTIVE** describing sausage.
- Pele only had to round the Chilean goalie and glide the ball into the net. **VERB.**
- The fox dodged round the hound and into the safety of a bramble thicket. **ADVERB** for it adds to, or modifies the verb 'dodged'.
- The guide ushered us round the palace. **PREPOSITION**. It could have been another preposition, 'into' 'past' or 'through' the palace.

I'll never forget that terrible fire even if it takes me the rest of my life to remember.

Nouns

Some facts about nouns. There are four kinds of nouns. These are:

- PROPER. Peter, Pauline, Petrograd, Picasso, Poland, all start with CAPITAL letter, no matter what you see in film or TV.
- COMMON. Everyday things – pin, pint, pan, pampas, pig, pigment, plum, psalm, people.
- ABSTRACT. Something you cannot touch or see like remorse, envy, love, joy, patience, greed, charity and ambition but the results of which are obvious.
- COLLECTIVE. As the name suggests, a collection of people or animals, such as class, team, herd, shoal, battalion, squad, usually treated as singular but sometimes plural. For example, Wyatt Earp is leading the *posse* of six men which *is* in hot pursuit of the cattle rustlers. Or, a *group* of scientists *is* on its way to Algeria to study the total eclipse of the sun. Watch if you start singular, keep to singular through the sentence. For example, "Italy has injected new blood into its team and they are expected to qualify for the World Cup finals." *Has* is singular and must be followed by the singular *it is* not *they are*.

Nouns can be either *singular* or *plural*. The plural is generally made by adding S or ES to the singular – *girl, girls*; *apple, apples; tomato, tomatoes*.

There are exceptions like *tooth, men* and *mouse,* and singulars ending in *U, A, O, I, X* and *Y*. If the dictionary does not give the plural, it means it ends normally in S. The dictionary also notes exceptions, like words ending in O, *pianos, potatoes, banjos* and also *banjoes*.

Adjective

An adjective describes or adds to the noun, e.g. *strong* tea, *healthy* diet, *those* Anglo Saxons, *your* turn, *foreign* coins, *worried* look, *shining* star.

Strong, healthy, those, your, foreign are the adjectives; *worried* and *shining* are adjectives that could also be verbs.

An adjective may not come immediately before a noun, but may be somewhere else in the sentence:

> The sky which had been cloudless a minute ago, turned dark and threatening.

The adjectives here are *cloudless, dark* and *threatening*.

Gender

Masculine for males, *feminine* for females, *common* for nouns like friend, cousin, doctor, priest or pilot, *neuter* for inanimate objects like door, pudding, ash and padlock.

Adverbs

Just as adjectives describe nouns, adverbs describe *verbs*, other *adverbs* and *adjectives*.

Most adverbs end in LY, e.g. quickly, gently, lovingly,

rudely, but not all words ending thus are adverbs. *Comely, lonely, lovely* are adjectives.

- "Read the question carefully before answering." *carefully* modifies the *verb read*.
- "Think very carefully before you answer.' VERY is the adverb describing the other adverb, *carefully*.
- "Bernadette took a very careful look before answering." Here *very* is an adverb describing the adjective *careful*.

Be careful now, *very* is not always an adverb!

- "Yes, Mum. I'll peel you a grape this very minute." Here, *very* is an adjective describing *minute*.

If you want to be grammatical, you could say that an adjective *qualifies* a noun and an adverb *modifies* a verb.

You could also avoid using an adjective as an adverb. For example,

"I could have run quicker but my feet were blistered during the race." This should be "I could have run more quickly....."

Comparison of Adjectives and Verbs

There are three degrees of comparison: positive, dealing with one person or thing; comparative, dealing with two; and superlative, comparing more than two.

Lesson Eight - Some Parts of Speech

- Angel Cabrera showed in the 2001 Masters that he is a *good* golfer. **Positive.**
- After his title fight with Barrera, Prince Naseem admitted the *better* man had won. **Comparative.**
- Before the season had finished, everyone knew the *best* team, Manchester United, would win yet another championship. **Superlative.**

Parse

To parse, means to tell what you know about the parts of speech. What happens if we parse the words in italics in the following sentences? Well, let us look at an example:

Columbus sailed off to discover America but only got *to Iona.*

Sailed –	verb, predicate of sentence.
Columbus –	proper noun, masculine, singular, nominative, subject to the verb sailed.
To –	preposition, governing the noun Iona in the objective case.
Iona –	noun, proper, singular, neuter, objective after the preposition *to*.

BC stands for Bing Crosby who was in that film with Freda Stair.

Exercise 8.1
Parse the following

Using the earlier example, try parsing the underlined words.

1. <u>I</u> promised my wee sister a <u>Barbie</u> doll for her <u>birthday</u>.
2. Dad painted our front <u>garden</u> gate while I <u>weeded</u> the vegetable <u>garden</u>.
3. <u>You</u> need perfect <u>balance</u> and a cool nerve to walk a tightrope <u>successfully</u>.
4. Willie Winn, <u>our</u> newest <u>and youngest</u> MP who had been ill, finally made his maiden speech today.

My wee brother rook the roll of the baker in the school play called pat a cake pat a cake.

Lesson Nine

Some More Grammar

Double Negative

It seems to be obligatory that crooks, cowboys and Corrie characters use only the double negative. "I ain't done nothin'," squawks the hitman, being chucked into the police van, meaning he had done nothing illegal. "It ain't nuthin' but beans," says the cowhand inviting the drifter to share a meal.

The double negative effectively says the opposite of what is intended. "I ain't done nuthin' " actually *means* "I have done something", not what was intended at all. It should be "I ain't done anythin'."

The John Wayne film *Comancheros* scored a treble negative. A country boy admiring a dandy's frilly shirt observes, "My ma had a fancy shirt. Never seen none on no man before."

This playground scenario might throw more light the double negative. Two close friends, Harry and Bruce, are arguing about a test tube Harry was using and was later found to be cracked:

Bruce:	"Imagine it, fined 50 pence for a test tube I didn't crack."
Harry:	"I'll lend you the 50 pence."
Bruce:	"Lend me! You should give me it."
Harry:	"Why?"

Bruce:	"You said nothing to old Papa Grieve."
Harry:	"I didn't"
Bruce:	"You didn't what?"
Harry:	"I did NOT say nothing. When I heard about you being fined, I went to him and told him you did not break the tube."
Bruce:	"And what did Papa say?"
Harry:	"Said somebody in the class broke it and it had to be paid for."
Bruce:	"Well thanks for not saying nothing."

Etcetera

When I was a teacher, I used to tell my class I would allow them to use etc. only once a year. A writer uses etc. to cover up his or her ignorance, or knows what to say or write, but is too lazy to do so.

etc is useful for things that are familiar to everyone. "Now this is our fifth holiday camp in France," says the Scoutmaster, "and you know to bring your passport, etcetera, etcetera."

Note the second line above,

"A writer uses etc. to cover his or her ignorance.."

Singular or Plural?

I use *his* or *her*, each of which is singular, to agree with the subject of the sentence, *writer* which is also singular. Most people would have written

"A writer uses it to cover up their ignorance."

Lesson Nine - Some More Grammar

Grammatically wrong for *their* is plural. Indeed, in such cases so many people do this that it will become correct usage, as English, a living language, accepts such change in time. This is a pity, for the sentence could have have been put in the plural from the start:

> "Writers use etc to cover up their ignorance..."

Granted it is a bit awkward using *his* or *her*, given our love of those short cuts.

However there can be no forgiveness for the experienced writer of sentence 13 (p ix) in the *Sunday Herald*, who wrote:

> "When you look into a person's eyes, you sometimes wonder what is going on in their head, especially if it is Richard Branson."

She starts with the singular, apostrophe before the S, and names the guy, the singular, masculine Richard Branson. Why murder the language? Put the shorter *his* instead of *their* and all is well. The same advice to the coach who proclaims,

> "Every one of my lads know this is the most important game of the season and they will all be doing their best."

There are no lassies in league football so he could start with "All my lads" or end with "doing HIS best."

Sentence 16 (p ix):

Agenda is the difference between men and women.

"The two neighbouring councils agreed in principal that in future their schools would not have seperate times for the Autumn holiday."

After *its* and *it's*, here are the next two most common howlers in English. *Separate* is the most commonly misspelt word in English, perhaps because we tend to pronounce it 'sepErate, and that's how we so often spell it. But it is *sep_a_rate*.

A *principal* is chief or head, say of a college, the number one:

The principal instigator of the Gunpowder Plot was not Guy Fawkes but Robert Catesby.

Principle means a fundamental truth, law, ideal or doctrine:

- The two councils agreed with the principle or idea of fairness that holidays should be at the same time to suit families from the district who had children at different council schools.
- The principle of steam power was discovered by Newcomen and improved by Watt.
- In 399BC, Socrates, the philosopher, was accused of corrupting the youth of Athens and rather than betray his principles and flee the city, drank the deadly cup of hemlock.

My mother is going to the dentist to get her teeth filed.

Lesson Ten

The Inelegant Sentence

Sentence 9 (p ix) is an example of inelegance or awkwardness:

> "It was through the instrumentality of Samuel Plimsoll and his Plimsoll Line and the idea saved the lives of countless seamen."

Instrumentality? Yes, there is such a word but it is in itself an inelegant word and is out of place. The conjunction *and* does not hold the sentence together and it must be rewritten. It is usual for *line* to start with a small *l*.

> It was because of Samuel Plimsoll and his line that many seamen's lives were saved.

Sentence structure can be complicated enough, so try to keep things simple and clear. Let's look at another example. Sentence 17 (p x) is also weak with its two *ands*:

> "The parachutist landed safely in the hay field and there were men working in it and they ran to help him."

Let's use *in which* then *and* to lock the words together:

- "A parachutist landed safely in the hayfield in

The gunman grabbed Charlie by the arm and poked a pistil in his ribs.

which men were working and ran to help." OR
- "The men working in a hayfield where a parachutist landed, ran to his help."

Sentence 9 (p ix) could also be improved:

> "When I first arrived in Lanarkshire, one was horrified at the smoke from factories and the awful pit bings practically in the town centres."

"One was horrified," change to "I was horrified..." to keep to same person as at the start, "When I first arrived..." I would also put the bit about the bings first, in case the reader got the idea that there was smoke from the bings as well as from the factories. There were many mining town and villages with pit bings, but only a few emitted smoke from buried burning coal. Also a comma after *factories*, showing that both bings and factories were in town centres:

> "When I first arrived in Lanarkshire, I was horrified at the awful pit bings and the smoke from factories, practically in the town centres."

Avoid using unecessarily complicated language when 'normal' language will do just as well. "I kept watch," explained the sleuth, "until 4 30am when the defendant made his exit from his place of abode." Nobody talks about their 'place of abode'? Why not simply, "until 4 30am when

---

A farmer in Wales runs his tractor on fuel he makes from pig manure and my Dad says I bet he calls it Shitty Shitty Bang Bang.

Lesson Ten - The Inelegant Sentence

the defendant came out of his house".

Councillors are usually a voluble lot. "These tenants of Glasgow council houses were ejected from their dwellings simply because they did not conform to the council's mandates with regard to the payment of their lawful responsibilities." You and I would say they were ejected because they did not pay the rent.

It is recommended we use ordinary words and phrases unless we want to be humorous or technical. Why tell us, "The automobile descended the declivity with increasing velocity" when it only means "the car increased its speed downhill"? Nor would we describe that careless motorist as *pococurante* (careless) even though the word is in the dictionary. Keep your sentence structures simple and avoid over-complicated things.

It was a gypsy woman that tolled my fortune at the garden fate.

Lesson Eleven

Metaphors and All That

Metaphors, similes and other figures of speech make speech and writing more colourful and varied.

A simile compares two unlike things that have something in common, and it is introduced by *as* or *like*. In WW11, a German general, Rommel was regarded by his enemy as *'cunning as a fox'* – a simile. Later he got the nickname, *'The Desert Fox'*, a metaphor. A metaphor, therefore is really a compressed simile, something which is used in place of something else. You could say "jealousy is like a green eyed monster" for the trouble it causes – a simile. Shakespeare wrote, "Jealousy, it is the green-ey'd monster." A metaphor. We might describe the singing of a lark as *wonderful*, but Shakespeare gets lyrical: "Hark, hark, the lark at heaven's gate." Robert Burns: "But pleasures are like poppies spread, you seize the flower, its bloom is shed." A simile using *like*.

Take a look at Sentence 18 on page x:

"It is strange the Conservatives have not privatised British Rail considering the vast amount of money being poured into its seemingly bottomless tunnel."

A bottomless tunnel? The Labour member was trying to make an apt metaphor by using *tunnel*, but was off track with bottomless. This is called a *mixed metaphor*.

"Everyone will be taking out their boats this Easter. The

air above may be warm but the water below is a different kettle of fish."

This is presumably a warning to sailors to be careful but flops by using *fish*. *Everyone* (singular) clashes with *their* (plural), and anyway, not everyone will be boating, only some of those with boats. This is a common assumption among sports writers. For example, "All eyes will be on Twickenham today when England take on France." No they won't, nor will *all eyes* in the coming months be on Wimbledon, Henley, Lords or St. Andrews.

A metaphor then is a figure of speech comparing two unlike things that have one feature in common, e.g. *"her golden hair was hanging down her back."* Hair and gold same colour. *"You are my sunshine, my only sunshine"*. You bring me the same joy as sunshine does. *"Shall I compare thee to a Summer's day?"* Shakespeare again.

Indeed, we use metaphors every day without our knowing it. *A pig in a poke, a land flowing with milk and honey*, a *wolf in sheep's clothing, a brass neck, silver hair*.

- "The SCWS (Scottish Co-operative Wholesale Society) may find itself on the losing end of the seesaw." Was the losing end the SCWS left high and dry, or was it brought crashing to earth?

- "I think there is a kind of swamp of up to 10 to 20 to 30 billions of waste in the Pentagon that can be ferreted out if you push hard enough." (US Budget Director, David Stockman.) A right fudger

---

Our Gertie hates chocolate moose.

is David the Director, anything between 10 to 30 billion and what's a mere billion? It's in a swamp that you can ferret out if you push hard enough. A treble mixed metaphor and David is awarded the trophy, Gift of the Gaffe.

A few other figures of speech worth a mention are categorised below.

Alliteration

Two or more words starting with the same letter or sound:

- Full fathom five your father lies and of his bones are coral made.
- A long line of lorries in a lamp lit lane.
- The ship carried a cargo of cedar wood, sandalwood and sweet white wine.

There is alliteration in the last point even though one word starts with 'c' and the next with 's', they sound similar and are followed by two with 'w'.

Personification

To ascribe a quality of a person to an inanimate object. *How sweet the moonlight sleeps upon this bank.* (Shakespeare again.) *I chatter, chatter as I flow. To join the brimming river; For men may come and men may go, but I go on forever.* (Tennyson, *The Song of the Brook*.)

Elephants trumpet because they go in bands.

Hyperbole

Hyperbole (*Hi-per-bo-lay*) is exaggeration for the sake of effect. *"Kiss me a thousand times"* (The Roman poet Catullus). *"An elegant blond with endless legs"* (Catrina Skepper in the *Daily Mail* TV programme)."*David Duchovy is out of this world*" (A film critic). T*he Sunday Times* recommends Janina, a 'humble' toothpaste at £8.95 that *"wipes the floor with the opposition."*

You may agree with me that 'humble' is exaggeration for a toothpaste that costs about three times as much as your ordinary tube and that 'wiping the floor' is rather an unhygenic and messy metaphor, even for a mixed one.

When my mum opened the steak and kidney pie it had nothing but sausages. My smarty sister said it was just a mistake but my smarty brother said it was an offal mistake.

Lesson Twelve

Sentence Joining

In Sentence 20 (p x), we touched on three ways of making good sentences. There is a fourth and we will look at the four in more detail.

> "General Custer carefully studied the surrounding territory. He immediately ordered the attack on the Indians.

Conjunctions

The most common way is to use a conjunction such as *and, but, though, although, while, because, so, since* and *if*. If the General had decided against an attack, the conjunction could be *and* or *but*:

> "General Custer studied the map of the surrounding territory but decided against an attack."

The reader may be left to deduce for himself why Custer so decided.

A conjunction may come at the start or the middle of the sentence.

After Easter Woolworths have a sale of Easter eggs, all shapes and sizes.

"Although the surrounding territory looked promising, General Custer decided against attacking the Indians."

"General Custer decided against attack since the territory did not look promising."

Relative Pronouns

Another joining ploy is the *relative pronoun*: *who, whose, whom, which, that* and occasionally, *what*. The relative pronoun is so called for it likes to be close to its relative in the sentence, and you will see in the three sentences below that *who* comes *immediately* after Napoleon, which is the *antecedent*. I well remember in Primary 6 our class learning these two big new words and being so chuffed that we bounded into the playground chanting, "The relative pronoun must come immediately after its antecedent."

Let's go into battle with another general, again using *who*:

- Napoleon was defeated at Waterloo. He was banished to St. Helena.
- Napoleon, *who* was defeated at Waterloo was banished to St. Helena. OR
- Napoleon, who was banished to St. Helena, had been defeated at Waterloo.

Reversing, that is putting the subject after the predicate, is another way of giving your sentences variety. The example is Shakespeare on page 46 where he is quoted,

---

My Grandad is crippled for he has the wrong kind of jeans.

> "Full fathom five thy father lies and of his bones are coral made."

We lesser mortals would have put it,

> "Your father lies five fathoms down and his bones have turned into coral."
>
> "More in hope than expectation of my team winning the cup did I go to the final that day."

The subject *I* and predicate *did go* are near the end.

Next, lets look at *whose*, which is used where there is the idea of possession, as in the following:

> **Oliver Twist** was born in the poorhouse.
> **His** mother had had no money or friends.

The relative pronoun must come immediately after its antecedent, and the story is about Oliver, so down goes his name first, Oliver, then the pronoun whose, followed naturally with mother.

> Oliver Twist, *whose* mother had no money or friends, was born in the poorhouse.

Here the possessive adjective *his* is replaced by the possessive relative pronoun *whose*.

- Ekaterina Furtseva was the only woman member of the presidium of the Soviet Union. *Her* visit to

---

Vincent O'Brien's 'Achieve' was beaten a head by 10-1 chance 'Kilian' yesterday at the Curragh It was impossible to separate them at the line.
(Source: The Herald, 1981)

Lesson Twelve - Sentence Joining

Britain in 1961 was to promote cultural exchange.

- Ekaterina Furtseva, *whose* visit to Britain in 1961 was to promote cultural exchange with Britain, was the only woman in the presidium of the Soviet Union.

Whom is needed when the subject changes, as below, from Mrs Takamoro to *you*:

Mrs. Takamoro is an expert in karate. *You* met her at the world ladies' championships.

Here are two subjects, Mrs. Takamoro and you. Start with *Mrs. Takamoro,* then *whom,* then *you,* then what you did...you met her...then the bit about Mrs. Takamoro:

Mrs Takamoro, *whom you* met at the world ladies championship, is an expert in karate.

Here's another example, this time with the relative pronoun *whom* near the end of the sentence:

Miss Plesh had just won Thunderball when she met Chick whom she married.

Which or *that* is used for inanimate objects like a car:

My dad bought a new Peugeot for our holiday in France. It broke down in the middle of rush hour traffic in Paris on the Champs Elysee.

Here, to use the relative pronoun, we will have to change

the order of the words to get *which* next to its antecedent:

> For our holiday in France, my dad bought a new Peugeot *which* (or *that*) broke down in the middle of rush hour traffic in Paris on the Champs Elysee.

Verb/Preposition Coupling

Verbs are sometimes used with a preposition, e.g. break through, recover from, listen to. You must use the preposition when joining sentences. For example,

- Scooby Doo had a bad attack of flu. He recovered *from* it only after a fortnight in bed.
- Scooby Doo had a bad attack of flu *from* which he recovered only after a fortnight in bed

Now let's look at when to use *what*.

- I never disbelieve what my best friend tells me.
- Miss Piggy is only doing what comes naturally.

Exercise 12.1
Using conjunctions and relative pronouns

Try joining these sentences either by a conjunction or by a relative pronoun. Remember, you can change the

---

Arthur looked great in his new blue suite at my sisters wedding.

Lesson Twelve - Sentence Joining

order of words, leave some out or add one or two.

1. The Pilgrim Fathers set sail for America in 1620. Their ship was called Mayflower.
2. The great storm raged two whole days. It destroyed thousands of trees all over the land.
3. Joan of Arc was born in the tiny village of Domremy. She led a French army against the English at the siege of Orleans.
4. Mozart wrote *The Magic Flute*. It is my favourite of all operas.
5. Mozart also composed *Figaro*. He died when he was only 36.
6. My Grandad won three prizes at the Bingo last night. His luck is fantastic.
7. That storm kept me awake all night. The papers hardly mentioned it.
8. Curly has a big telescope up in his attic. He looks through it each night to study the stars.
9. Al Jolson was born Asa Yoelson in Russia. He became a famous singer and film star in the United States. He appeared in the first all talking picture, *The Jazz Singer,* in 1927.
10. When I heard an actor say, "Did they saw their way through?" I thought at first it was bad grammar. Seconds later I realised he was a detective investigating a burglary.

At the circus in Wishaw it cost the crowd sixpence to see lovely Laura and her huge loins.

Lesson Thirteen

More About the Sentence

Let's look at a few more issues dealing with sentences and sentence structure.

Phrase in Apposition

The phrase "now a favourite in Britain" is meaningless on its own, but if put with other words they become very meaningful:

> The tasty pizza, *now a favourite in Britain*, is Italian in origin.

The sentence could also be written:

> *Italian in origin*, the tasty pizza is now a favourite in Britain.

The phrase in aposition is now "Italian in origin", and it must have a following comma.

The phrase in aposition gives variety to writing, and is useful in forming long sentences. For example, the following sentences can be made into one long one using this technique:

> Thomas Carlyle was a Scotish historian
> He was born in Ecclefechan in Dumfriesshire.
> He wrote the famous *History of the French Revolution*.

He is nicknamed 'The Sage of Chelsea'.

Using the phrase "the Scottish historian and nicknamed "The Sage of Chelsea' as the phrase in apposition, the joined sentence becomes:

Thomas Carlyle, *the Scottish historian and nicknamed 'The Sage of Chelsea'*, was born in Ecclefechan, Dumfriesshire, and is famous for his work *The History of the French Revolution*.

Participle Phrases, Present and Past

Like the phrase in apposition above, present and past participle phrases are words that make no sense on their own. "Seizing hold of his fishing net" is useless unless we add something like a farmer catching his runaway turkey:

Seizing hold of his fishing net, Farmer Ticklebaum rushed out to capture his runaway prize turkey.

The phrase in italics is present tense, and is a *present participle phrase*. The farmer catches his bird, which we can describe in the past tense with a past participle phrase:

Having caught his turkey, he locked it up in his bedroom.

Five kinds of sentence

There are five kinds of sentence – *short, long, simple, compound, complex.*

A ***short*** sentence may have but one word, *Halt! Hurry!* where the subject *You* is understood. It may be two words, like, *"Arsenal won.."* Or more, *"Arsenal won the league and cup double in 1997."* This is also a simple sentence with one subject, Arsenal and one predicate, won, with the league and cup double an extension of the predicate. An extension of a subject or predicate just means telling more about it. However, a simple sentence could also be a ***long*** one:

> "Colin Montgomerie, a native of Troon, familiar with the course since boyhood and son of the secretary, is hoping for success in the forthcoming British Open at the beginning of June."

One subject, *Colin Montgomerie*. One predicate, *is hoping*.

Good writing is a mixture of the five kinds of sentences. Too many short sentences may give a staccato effect, and many long sentences could be boring and hard to follow. Here is an example from the *Daily Mail*:

> "The stewards, chaired as on September 19th by Tim Martin-Holland who has been asked to appear before the Jockey Club's Disciplinary Committee for a briefing on the lack of action over Silken Dalliance's running, asked themselves whether Eddry tried to get into the race."

The subject is the stewards, then Tim gets into the act, but further on is the predicate, asking themselves if Eddry had tried to get into the race. But Tim was being asked by the Jockey Club about the stewards' lack of action on Eddry's riding of Silken Dalliance. A case of the journalist forgetting who was the subject by the time he got to

---

Czar and kaiser come from Caesar and none of the three were up to much in history.

> ### Exercise 13.1
> ## Completing Sentences
>
> Complete the following with appropriate sentences. Try to make them interesting. A lazy writer would be content with "she fell to the ground." Not very interesting! Think about a name in history, fiction, the news, a hero or heroine.
>
> 1. Gasping for breath...
> 2. Having no money in her purse...
> 3. Not knowing the...
> 4. Having thought the matter over...
> 5. Having reached the oasis....
> 6. Without having had her...

the end of his sentence. This long sentence could have read simply,

> "Chief steward Tim Martin-Holland has been asked by the Jockey Club if any inquiry had been made into Eddry's riding of Silken Dalliance."

A *compound* sentence has been formed from two or more simple sentences.

> Sandra loves tripe and onions. Sanny hates tripe and onions.

Join them to get a compound sentence:

> Sandra loves tripe and onions but Sanny detests them.

Two subjects, Sandra and Sanny. Two predicates, loves and detests. The sentences may be longer:

> Sandra loves tripe and onions especially when she makes the dish at home with the finest ingredients but Sanny hates tripe and onions even when his mother cooks them.

A ***complex*** sentence has at least one independent clause and at least one subordinate clause. *"Because the crew mutinied"* is such a phrase, or subordinate clause, that needs an independent clause to make sense:

> Captain Bligh failed to deliver the breadfruit plants because the crew mutinied

One independent clause, *Captain Bligh failed to deliver the breadfruit plants*. One subordinate clause, *because the crew mutinied*. You could have two independent clauses and two subordinates. *Captain Bligh who failed to deliver breadfruit to England because the crew mutinied, was furious and promised that every mutineer would be caught and (that every mutineer would be) hanged from the highest yardarm in Portsmouth*. Two independent clauses and four subordinates:

> [Independent] Captain Bligh was furious, and (Captain Bligh) promised
> [Subordinates] who failed to bring bread fruit to England
> because the crew mutinied that every mutineer would be caught

---

Nicholas Fairbairn writes an appreciation of Sir Ian Moncrieff of that Ilk who died yesterday the age of 63, on page 11.

Lesson Thirteen - More About the Sentence

and that every mutineer would be hanged from the highest yardarm in Portsmouth.

To sum up, acceptable writing will have a mix of short, long, simple, compound and complex sentences, firmly constructed by conjunctions, relative pronouns, phrases in apposition and participle phrases.

Later we shall see the importance of vocabulary, that is the correct nouns, adjective, verbs, adverbs and figures of speech.

Write a sentence about Yokohama.
"She married one of the Beatles."

Exercise 13.2
Sentence Structure

Have a go at using different methods of sentence construction for at least some of the twelve sentences given below.

1. Soapy was in a bad mood. Someone had turned on a bunsen burner before leaving the science room.
2. Smartypants Yogi Bear dearly loved 'picknic' baskets. He sneaked them out of tourists' cars. The park ranger nearly always caught him. He had to hand the baskets back. He had to apologise.
3. Michelangelo was a poet, painter, sculptor, architect and engineer. Many historians consider him to be the cleverest man ever.
4. Minnehaha O'Toole was a Wishaw washerwoman. Her daughter once climbed every greasy pole in the state of Wisconsin.
5. In Dumfriesshire near the Bellybought Hill is the little village with the littlest name, Ae. The BBC Dictionary of Pronunciation declares it rhymes with *day*.
6. This film is about a gigantic Caribbean octopus. With its 19 metre long tentacles, it crunches every wooden ship. These ships are carrying slaves. They are intended for the undersea king-

---

The will of an Irish shirt maker was found in the pocket of a pair of trousers he had sent to cleaners three years after his death.

Lesson Thirteen - More About the Sentence

dom of Atlantica.
7. Alexandre Gustave Eiffel was a French engineer. He designed the famous tower for the Paris Exhibition of 1898. For many years it was the highest man made structure on earth.
8. The undercover police moved into the open air Saturday market. They arrested three members of a cigarette gang. One of them punched a policeman and escaped.
9. Aunt Jemima is 87 years old. She does not look her age. Her favourite pastime is crotcheting napkins and doyleys. She gives them to relatives and friends at Christmas.
10. Sodium is a very corrosive metal. Chlorine is a very poisonous gas. The two unite to form sodium chloride. This is the very substance we know as salt.
11. The world is tilted at an angle of $23^{1/2}°$. This gives us the Tropic of Cancer and the Tropic of Capricorn. In Britain, it also gives us unequal day and night and the four seasons.
12. Prince Aloysius was told a 40 foot dragon was terrorising the villagers. He grabbed his bumbag. He fearlessly confronted the beast. He knew dragons liked porridge and threw it lumps of cold porridge laced with sassafras oil which rendered it as docile as Larry The Lamb.

When I grow I am goin to be a teaser and learn the boys 2 wun are 2.

Lesson Fourteen

Tense

Tense means you may not say or write *I done, I have did, I seen, I have saw, I have went* or *I swum*. These are the mortal sins of grammar. Table 1 on page 64 will help with these and other verbs.

Active and Passive

Did you know verbs have voices? They have two, active and passive, and this gives further variety to your writing.

Dan McGrew won the slow bike race at Auchensuggle.

You remember, of course, the three parts of a sentence, subject predicate and object.

In passive voice, the sentence is reversed so the subject, Dan McGrew, becomes the object. The objective, the slow bike race at Auchenshuggle, becomes the subject:

- The slow bike race at Auchenshuggle was won by Dan McGrew.

Here are some more reversals from the active to the

Marie Antoinette could not have said Let them eat cake for the Paris bakers were on strike.

passive voice:

- Henry VIII wore these garters. *These garters were worn by Henry VIII.*
- I was stung by a bee. *A bee stung me.*
- An angel visited Abou Ben Adam during the night. *Abou Ben Adam was visited by an angel during the night.*

Transitive and Intransitive Verbs

You have been using these, though not by name. You know about subject, predicate and object in a sentence and that some verbs need help (an object) to make sense. "He hit...."whom or what did he hit? He hit me, *me* is objective after the transitive verb *hit*. "He hit the target." Target is in the objective case too.

Transitive comes from the same Latin word for transport, to carry and you do carry on from the transitive verb to the object. *Larks sing, bees sting, an alsatian barks, my mum narks.* These verbs need no object and are intransitive.

The sports page may have the headline, "New York Yankees win!" *Win* is intransitive here. Or, "The Yankees win the World Series!" Here *win* is transitive, as it takes us from one part of the sentence to the next.

It could happen that a verb could be transitive or intransitive, depending on the work it does in a sentence. Remember the word *round* that could be a noun, adjective, verb, adverb and preposition.

Kruschev is leader of the Germans and only has to touch a button to blow up the hole world.

Table 1 - Verbs and tense

Verb	Past tense	Present tense
begin	I began	I have begun
bite	I bit	I have bitten
come	I came	I have come
do	I did	I have done
drink	I drank	I have drunk
forget	I forgot	I have forgotten
go	I went	I have gone
eat	I ate	I have eaten
hang (a picture)	I hung	I have hung
know	I knew	I have known
to lie (down)	I lay	I have lain
to lie (fib)	I have lied	I lied
rise	I rose	I have risen
shake	I shook	I have shaken
speak	I spoke	I have spoken
spell	I spelt spelled	I spelt or spelled
spring	I sprang	I have sprung
steal	I stole	I have stolen
swell	it swelled	it has swollen
swim	I swam	I have swum
tell	I told	I have told
write	I wrote	I have written
wear	I wore	I have worn

It was hard luck Douggie could not eat his free dinner as he had an abess in his mouth.

Exercise 14.1
Active to Passive

- The wind blew down our tent and a whippet scoffed our corn beef sandwiches.
- Louis Bleriot flew the Channel in 1909 and Lindbergh the Atlantic in 1927.
- Our wee Benny did not break Ginty's window.
- Partick Thistle offered us free tickets for Wednesday's big game.
- The winning goal in the World Cup final was snatched by Big Andy Gump.

General degoal was the one that did not want Britain to join the Budget.

Lesson Fifteen

Through the Alphabet

This lesson takes you through many other of the most common grammatical mistakes.

Affect & Effect

Affect is a verb, as in:

> "It is feared that the outbreak of foot and mouth disease will affect racing in Britain and even cancel Cheltenham."

Effect is a noun:

> "Many parents are worried about the effect of the MMR inoculation on their children."

Aggravate & Irritate

Irritate means to anger or annoy, and aggravate is to make matters worse.

> "At first her cough was only irritating but she aggravated it by going out in her slippers to hang up the washing."

Altar & Alter

When I was teaching, I saw a colleague had written

Lesson Fifteen - Through the Alphabet

> "The High Priest led the sacrificial lamb to the alter."

on the blackboard. I did not wish to embarrass him in the classroom so did not suggest he alter *alter* to *altar*:

> "Ferdy the forger skilfully altered the cheque from £1,900 to £4,900."

Awful

"The only time to use 'awful' is in describing the Day of Judgement." A warning from a teacher of English. Today he would add dropping an atom bomb. Exaggeration, perhaps, but it did make us treat the word with caution.

> "An awful lot of new restaurants have have opened in Brussels with the influx of so many Eurocrats,"

a newspaper heading that would have been clearer simply with *'Many new restaurants'*.

A Total Of

TV reports on the closure of another textile mill in the Borders.

> "It is feared a total of 250 jobs will go."

Why *a total of* when 250 would do? A common redundancy.

Bonus

Bonus is something for which you do not pay. It might be two Kit Kats for the price of one. So the wording on the packet is verbosity, Extra Free or Free Bonus Kit Kat is a bit too much. Free or bonus would suffice.

Because

Use it without *reason* or *why*. So often you read

> "The reason why I do not like you is because you are a stingy bugger."

It would be better as:

> "The reason I do not like you is that you are a stingy bugger." Or:
> "I do not like you because you are a stingy bugger."

Both

What need is there for *both* in:

> "I know both him and his wife and like the two of them"?

You could also ask the same about *the two of them*. Not very mannerly to put *him* first:

> "I know her and her husband and like them."

Clichés

I feel anyone who uses these is lazy and without imagination. A cliché is a phrase that was hailed with delight because it was catchy but has become tired and worn with

Lesson Fifteen - Through the Alphabet

use. You would not wear someone else's cast off socks!

Listen to politicians on TV and it will be surprising if they don't come away with, *"At this moment in time," "at the end of the day," "no way," "you know"* or *"moving the goalposts"*. Here are some of the *top of the pops* at this *particular moment in time*!

At this juncture, at this juncture in time
Each and every one
Without further ado
With these few words
It is a privilege and a pleasure
Having said that
In my humble opinion
Far be it for me
Without fear or favour
I shudder to think
In this day and age

It is interesting to note how successive dictionaries treat the word cliché:

Webster 1895. A stereotype plate.
Chambers 1906. Not mentioned.
Reader's Digest 1964. Stereotype or electrotype block; stereotyped or commonplace phrase or expression.
Chambers 1967. An electrotype or stereotype plate; a hackneyed phrase.
Collins 1977. Word or expression that has lost much of its force through over exposure.

The working class is not allowed to be an MP.

Continual & Continuous

Continual is lasting over a period, minutes to years, with frequent stops:

> "Simple Simon complained that Smokey Sam upstairs was learning the banjo and the continual plonking over nine months was driving him mad."

Continuous is used for over a period without ceasing:

> "The nine hours continuous rain was enough to flood the half of Perth."

Disinterested & Uninterested

At a trial the judge must be *disinterested*, meaning he must not take sides either with the prosecution or the defence, but he will not be *uninterested* in the court proceedings.

Neither & Either

Either is always followed by or, as follows: *"Either you eat those prunes or you get no disco money."* Neither always takes nor, as follows: *"There was neither manna nor water for the Israelites in the desert."*

Euphemism

A nicer way of saying something unpleasant. Being dead: from *"in the bosom of the Lord"* to *"In His keeping"*, to the less reverent *"kicked the bucket"*. Telling lies is being *"economical with the truth,"* *'downsizing'* for laying you off, *'waste disposal officer'* for the bin man, and Mr Clinton's relationship with Miss Lewinsky is officially called *'inappropriate.'*

In the film, *It's a Mad, Mad, Mad, Mad World*, the euphemistic and the literal were combined in the shot of a victim kicking a bucket in his dying spasms.

Fewer or Less

Fewer is an adjective and less an adverb, sometimes an adjective.

- "My dad has been ordered by the doctor to smoke less." Less is an adverb modifying smoke.
- "My dad has been ordered to smoke less tobacco" adjective qualifying tobacco.
- "My Dad has been told to smoke fewer cigars". Fewer, an adjective describing cigars.

QUANTITY (Less)	NUMBERS (Fewer)
traffic	cars
crime	criminals
land	fields
trouble	riots
housing	houses

Constantinople is now called East And Bull.

Congratulations to Safeway who recently changed the express check out notice from less than nine to fewer than nine.

First & Priority

Two words meaning the same. First is first and priority is first. If you get priority at the airport, you will be first on to the plane. Politicians babble about "first priority" when it should simply be, "My priority will be..."

Fortuitous

Does not mean lucky but that something occurred by chance. Thus,

> "it was fortuitous for Mr Seminola when a chance vistor informed him that the heavy vase acting as a door stopper was a Ming vase from the umptheenth dynasty, probably worth half a million".

Fudging

Fudgers will not give a straight answer and are evasive because they are not sure of their facts or steadfast in their opinions. In a TV book programme, one critic stated,

> I rather tend to be of the opinion that his latest book may not be quite up to the standard of his earlier work.

The Great fire of London was a good thing in a way for it burnt Guy Fox.

Note the quibble words, *rather, tend, may* and *quite*. She could have said, "I do not think (rather than, 'I tend to be of the opinion') this book is as good as his earlier one."

Archie McPherson at Tynecastle.

> "The Hearts' goalkeeper, Cruickshanks clearly appeared to be bundled into the net but the referee gave Celtic a goal."

Oh Archie, '*clearly appeared*!'

From a prepared speech, "*Things, objects, were flying about in the air....*" He was describing a riot at a football match he had attended in Montevideo. But what was flying through the air? Coins, cushions, stones, bottles, golf balls, bongo bongo drums? You cannot get away with vague statements in a speech or exam. And how did a pupil of mine expect to get away with, "*The Magna Carta came out in 1216, 1213 or 1220.*" No luck. Minnie, it was 1215.

Fulsome

Fulsome is fawning, not genuine. If the second violinist heaps fulsome praise on the conductor, he is looking for promotion.

Get & Got

In speech, at least, two of the most used and abused words in English. *Get up, get dressed, get married, get divorced, got my degree, got a haircut, got a hernia*. Good and useful words but so monotonous, especially in writing. Consider this composition:

> "I was shopping to get a first aid outfit and in The

Emporium got into the lift to get to the fourth floor but only got to the third when it shook a bit and got stuck. Naturally I pressed the fourth button but it did not move. I tried again but it did not get started. I never got such a fright in my life especially when I could not get the door to open. By this time a small group of shoppers got around the lift and one of them went to get an attendant but it was a good ten minutes before he appeared and got the gate to open and I got out and got my breath back. It was a long time before I ever got into another lift in The Emporium or anywhere else, I can tell you."

Quite an adventure, but spoiled by so many *gots*. How about:

"I went shopping to The Emporium for a first aid kit on the fourth floor. I took an empty lift but it shuddered to a stop at the third. Naturally, I pushed the fourth button but the lift moved not. What a fright when I found the door would not open. By this time a group of shoppers had gathered and one signalled he was going for help but it was a long ten minutes before an attendant appeared, I was near the edge of panic. Yes, you may be sure it was a long time before I used the lift at The Emporium or anywhere else."

Not a 'get' or a 'got' in sight, and far more interesting to hear about.

There are dye works in Perth because if you have a red coat you can get it blue.

Half

"The upside down cake has two halves which means they are equal so you canny give the wee half to Juliette and wolf the big half," my dear Watson. A half is a half, so you can't have a big or a small half!

Incredible & Incredulous

Incredible refers to facts, incredulous to people:

> I'm looking out the window and what do I see? Incredibly, the road is being patched up by the council.

> 'It was announced to an incredulous audience that Pavarotti was taking over from Tom Jones'.

Learn & Teach

You can learn or teach yourself Esperanto but cannot learn others. A former pupil had me blushing with her compliments on how good I had learnt her English. I thought I had learned her better than that!

Looseness

The parts of a sentence should be *integrated*, that is they should have a feeling of relationship. *"Sir Francis Drake, returned to a hero's welcome in England and did not reveal the*

It was during the Crime war that balaclavas were discovered.

fortune he had plundered from the Spaniards." Both statements are informative, but you have the feeling that the first would have had something about the Spaniards or the Queen. *'But'* after England or *'who'* after Drake leaving out *'and'* would be better.

> "The chairman of FIXIT, the giant DIY firm, he is called Sir Iggy O'Higgins, is to retire next month".

Omit *'he is called'* as a sentence does not need two subjects..

> "I have come to the same conclusion about the transfer that you do."

There is discomfort about the change from *'have'* to *'do'*. Better using *'have'* at the end.

Lumps

> "The builders were busy building a large building."

This is an obvious example of lumpy writing, the repetition of the same or similar sounding words in a sentence or in a nearby sentence. It can easily avoided with a little thought.

> "The workers were busily putting up a new mosque."

Naming the building enriches the sentence and may cause the reader, for example, to find something about mosques or Islam.

Anyone born near Bow bells is called a cockney like Bo Peep.

"The affair of the Ayr dog, condemned for barking at a postman, is very unfair."

Here you have sound similarity in *Ayr, affair* and *unfair*.

"President Carter made a very statesmanlike statement."
General Luntz, NATO commander.

Why not have a shot at recasting the above two sentences?

Nice

The most overworked word in the business. Like *get* and *got* it is all right in daily chit-chat but not in writing or speechmaking. *A nice haggis, holiday, friend, dress, sunset, film, bus driver*. No no. *A tasty haggis, relaxing holiday, trusty friend, fashionable dress, glorious sunset, thrilling film, helpful bus driver*. Yes, yes, that's better.

Non-existent Words

Irregardless and independant – the first is *regardless* and the second *independent*. There is the noun *dependant*. "My dad gets tax relief for his dependants, my brother and me." Nor may you say *dependant on someone or something*. The word is *dependent*.

Listenable – "*His speech was listenable.*" Listenable sounds

---

Joan of Arc married a Roman and when he died they wanted his money back but she said I'll give you half but they wanted it all so she rose up and slautered them but Caesar raised an army and she fled to the hills.

a good word but it ain't. Nor are *hearable, ginormous* or *shambolic* in the dictionary (yet).

Only

Careful where you put *only* in a sentence. It ought to come next to or as close to the word it is meant to affect.

"Micawber was only trying to cheer up David."

is not the same as

"Only Micawber was trying to cheer up David".

> Try putting *only* into various places in this sentence:
> *Dickie's auntie sent him a fiver for passing his exam.*

Personally

"When I say this, I am speaking personally and I feel the council tax must go up."

A councillor is making sure he is not voicing the will of the council. One of his constituents interviewed on TV may declare

"Personally speaking, I think the tax is too high."

He need not use *personally speaking* because the viewers know

---

The Pilgrim Fathers crossed the Atlantic to follow cod in their own way.

he is expressing only a personal opinion. A Scots singing star, Sidney Devine's TV advert, "*Every song personally chosen by Sidney Devine himself.*" No need for *personally* or *himself*.

Practice & Practise

Without doubt, the most common written error.

Practice is a noun – the doctor's *practice*. Nigel Kennedy did endless *practice* before he became a famous violinist. It is the conjurer's *practice* to tell jokes while performing.

Practise is a verb – a medical student has to *practise* taking blood pressure. Nigel Kennedy has to *practise* for hours every day. The conjurer *practises* telling jokes.

- "North Lanarks Council did not close the dirty café as it was not their practise..". Wrong!
- "It's queer the dentist was allowed to continue practicing after he was reported." Wrong!

The problem may be that the words are pronounced similarly. If we think of *advice* the noun and *advise* the verb when we are using *practice* and *practise*, it could keep us right.

> C = the noun. Practice advice
> S = the verb. Practise advise.

What is the opposite of vacant? 'Engaged'. Give the opposite of find. 'Not guilty'.

Pronoun Use

Remember how hard it is sometimes to get the right pronoun at the end of a sentence? Is it *I* or *me, him* or *her*? The table below should help.

Table 2 - Pronouns

	Subject (nominative case)	**Object** (objective case)
First person, singular	I	me
Second person, singular	you	you
Third person, singular	he, she, it	him, her, it
First person, plural	we	us
Second person, plural	you	you
Third person, plural	they	them

Shapes & Colours

A square is a square and does not need *shape*:

- "It is an unusual button being square in shape."
- "The garden design is oval in shape."
- "Our maths teacher could draw a perfect circle freehand."

Perfect is unnecessary in the latter, for it would not be a cir-

---

Pros and cons is from America where it means golfers and convicts.

cle if its radius was not uniform. That dress is not red in colour, it is just red. *"To get green, mix the colours blue and yellow.* Leave out *the colours*; it's unnecessary.

Slang

There'a no objection to slang (*skint, duds, fags, bonkers, jammy*) in everyday speech, but not in writing unless in a story or quoting someone.

Their and There

Their is a possessive adjective like *my, your, his, her,* so it will be followed by a noun, e.g. *their money, their hopes, their holidays, their mistakes, their parents.*

There is no such word as, *their's, her's, mine's, your's*. No apostrophe, thank you.

There contains the other word that is so closely associated with *it, here, a spot, a place, a position. Wait there, wait here. There is the answer, here is the answer.* There is not followed by a noun. When reading, note how the writer uses here and there and you will gradually get used to the difference between the two words.

Unrelated Participle

This must relate to the subject of the sentence that follows, e.g.

Coming up the hill, the town clock struck midnight

This is wrong, because the sentence must say who is coming up the hill – the poacher, the parson, Corocodile Dunbar.

Coming up the hill, Crocodile Dunbar heard the clock strike midnight.

Very

"The bullets went through the ceiling which was very undamaged."

This must be a printer's error for it is impossible to see what *very* is doing in the sentence.

"Yashikomo, the Japanese golfer, is very unknown in this country!"

What's the difference between being *unknown* and *very unknown*?

"The games master says that Antoinette ran a very excellent race."

It seems to me that *very* detracts from the forceful word *excellent* as you cannot put emphasis on *excellent*.

"It would be a very good idea if TV gave you time to copy e-mail numbers."

Here *very* strengthens the weaker adjective *good*, and is used correctly.

Words Commonly Mispronounced

- **Genuine** rhymes not with *wine* but with *in*, gen-u-in.
- **Heinous** meaning awful, "drug dealing is a heinous

Lesson Fifteen - Through the Alphabet

(<u>hay - nus</u>) crime".
- I trust you will never be indicted (<u>in-dited</u>) for dangerous driving.
- Remember the first *R* in <u>February</u>.
- <u>Um-brella</u> not *umb<u>e</u>r-ella*.
- In mischievous, the accent is on the first syllable, <u>mis-che-vus</u>.
- In harass the accent is on the first syllable. <u>Har-ass</u>.

The three natural regions of Scotland are the hemisfear the clyde and glasgow.

Lesson Sixteen

Spelling

English spelling is, to say the least, a bit maddening. Five letters for a word that needs only one, *queue*, *tar* for the stuff used in road building, but *ptarmigan*, the game bird. *Awesome* but leave out the 'e' in *awful*, *fire* but *fiery*, *humour* but *humorous*, omitting the second 'u', *murder* but *murderous*, *disaster* but *disastrous*, *bosom* with the two o's sounded differently. *Bear* and *bare*, *beech* and *beach*, *eye*, *ewe* and *yew*, look different but sound the same. It is not the exotic words that bemuse us.

At school we did experiments using *ipecacuanha* and *phenolphthalein* and I remember to this day how to spell them. It is the supposedly simple words that has me guessing. Are there two m's in *accommodation*, two c's in *acoustics*, one or two n's in *planning*?

I think it best to learn the spelling of the words we are most likely to use daily, and these are in the list below, words I corrected hundreds of times in my 40 years in the classroom. (Separate is in bold for it has the distinction of being the most abused word in English.)

accommodation	beautiful	conscious
apartment	business	conscience
Arctic	catalogue	crescent
Antarctic	ceiling	design
Autumn	cheque	develop
awkward	committee	different
believe	colour	envelope

Lesson Sixteen - Spelling

disease	idle	receipt
disappear	irresistible	receive
disappoint	knowledge	reign
doctor	lightning	**separate**
electricity	mischievous	sincerely
embarrass	medicine	skilful
February	muscle	succeed
flu	needle	tongue
friend	oblige	truly
fulfil	occasion	until
gauge	occurred	unusual
guess	parliament	weather
government	peaceful	whether
handle	poisonous	Wednesday
harass	precede	width
eight	proceed	yolk
humorous	recipe	

The battle of a La Main was the end of Rommell the dessert fox

Lesson Seventeen

Words that Work

The French have a phrase, *le mot just*, the right word. We must do the same in English and find the right word, the word we need to express ourselves exactly. We have plenty of help in the dictionary, in the thesaurus and in our heads if we think hard enough.

Let's suppose you are a girl with a clumsy brother who, at breakfast, drops an egg spoon that lands on your foot. If some of the egg bespatters your shoe you might be *vexed* but no more than that if you can easily wipe it off. However, the egg is runny, and some seeped into your foot and you are *annoyed* you have to leave the table to clean up. But you are wearing your prized satin slippers and the egg leaves a stain, which *angers* you. If he drops a heavy hammer on your toes and you cannot go to the class Hallowe'en party, you are *furious*. *Le mot just*, a word for every occasion.

Vexed, annoyed, angry, furious are words arranged in order of strength. It's the same with other everyday words, nouns, adjectives. That big brother can *tease, chaff, bother, badger, pester, irritate, plague* and *torment*. People don't just walk, but *strut, stroll, saunter, stride, toddle, tramp, trample, amble, promenade* and *shuffle*. They not only talk but *murmur, hiss, drawl, bawl, stutter, mutter, whisper, sneer, scoff, wail, respond, reply* and *scold*.

Agony! Anguish! Horror! Nightmare! Chaos! Reports on an earthquake, a plane crash, an M1 pile up, a hotel fire? No! All these were used in editions of the *Daily Mail*, (although it could be any daily blatt) about Scotland being eight players short for the World Cup against Estonia. Just a wee bit hysterical you might muse, over a football match.

Chaos? Scottish teachers might strike if they don't get more time to deal with the proposed new Leaving Certificate exam, Higher Still. I can't wait to ask my granddaughter, who's in fifth year, if the teachers are sulking in the staff room and the pupils prancing over the desk tops.

You might also be wondering what words the journalists can come up with to describe a really tragic accident It reminds me of the advent of the *talkies* many years ago and the cinema trailers for forthcoming films: *Stupendous! Gigantic! Colossal! Fantastic! Awesome! Glittering!* However, the wordsmiths have come to the rescue of today's copywriters with the prefixes *super*, then *multi*, then *hyper* and now *Mega*. Wonder what they will come up with next. Can you think of one?

That *big* man may be big in build or a genius or wealthy or powerful politically or just a tall, really nice bloke, kind, gentle and good natured. Big also describes a multitude of nouns from a garden to a desert, a pizza to a banquet. There are over a hundred synonyms for *fool* in Roget's thesauras, and 40 for *mischievous*. These words are not reserved for novelists, playwrights and poets, but for you and me. Let's use them, *les mots justs*

When things are not going well with you everything seems to be against you.
BBC Radio on West Ham.

Exercise 17.1
Word strength

You might like to put these words in ascending order of 'strength'.

1. small, infinitesimal, minute, microscopic.
2. big, large, vast, colossal.
3. furious, livid, annoyed, irritated.
4. brutal, harsh, stringent, rigorous.
5. skelletal, lean, shrunken, skinny.
6. bolt, hasten, sprint, trot.
7. scallywag, villain, imp, rascal.
8. hilarious, droll, funny, side-splitting.
9. delighted, ecstatic, satisfied, pleased.
10. glum, sad, dejected, melancholic.

Four towns founded by the Romans are Bath, Bathgate, Blackpool and Liverpool.

Lesson Eighteen

For Amusement Only

Collecting grammatical and other mistakes from the media is good fun, and they need not be howlers in English, but unusual items like the rugby result *"Scotland under 21, 21 England under 21, 21."*

Here are a few I have collected from the press.

- Fracas outside inn. (Punchup outside pub)
- Highway Cod. (Fish lorry overturns on M74)
- Woof Proof Roof. (Police dog kennels roofed over after residents complain about the dogs barking.)

This mangled advert appeared in the run up to Christmas:

"Wishaw Co-Operative Funeral Society. Book your place now before it is too late. Accommodation limited.

In two successive weeks in November 2002, the following adverts appeared:

HGV 1 night drunk driver. Monday to Friday from Wishaw to Litchfield

Shotts Prison. Time served joiner required.

From the Engagements column:

Both families are pleased to announce the engagement of Geenamay, eldest daughter of Tam and Leetitia Prester to Alex and Amanda Faieworth.

Also on sale are wellies designed for Jackie Stewart's shop at Gleneagles Hotel, lined with Stewart tartan. (Source: *Sunday Times*, 1989.)

Have you ever seen a tartan-lined shop before?!

- Brigadier Gerard will attempt to gain in the King George and Queen Elizabeth Stakes, his 15th win in a row without defeat. (Source: Peter O'Sullivan, racing commentator.)

- My marker was close to me so I fainted right and swung left. This have me the space to shoot and score. (A Joe Harper goal but not his spelling. Source: *Sunday Mail*, 1981.)

- Cash book banned at Wimbledon! (The tennis wallahs do not care for some of the contents of Pat Cash's memoirs.)

- "It's behind you, David!" (*Daily Record* photo of the ball the English goalie missed against Brazil. Perhaps like me, you see a double entendre. Not only is the ball behind him but also the World Cup.)

The 'in-word' at the moment (summer 2002) is 'poised':

"Rangers poised to sign new faces".

You might wonder how you sign a face!

Lesson Eighteen - For Amusement Only

- The Chancellor poised to present his budget.
- Scottish MPs poised to vote themselves salary increase.
- Henman poised to win his first title in Paris.

A new word, *Telegaffes*, from howlers in TV subtitles:

- It's a pity the cue ball had to Rick O'Shea off the yellow and into the pocket.
- If this young Frenchman on the last tee at Carnoustie wins the Open, it will be a great boost for the game of government.
- Sie James Barrie is the July in the crown of Scottish literature.
- Several rockets were fired in Islamabad yesterday. It is thought that were aimed at American tarts in the city.
- Republicans want the hand count in three Florida districts Cannes Selled.
- The votes in the House of Lords are being counted, eyes to the fight, nose to the left.
- Americans are both confused and bewildered at what's happening in the Presidential elections.
- She is the proud grandmother of a son she has never seen.
- The Renaissance was at the beginning of the modern world as we know it today.

- If things go on as they are doing, the musk ox will face distinction within 30 years.

- For years now, we have been dropping poison into the eyes of rabbits are other maiden speakers.

- "We are raising money for the sammary tones." Marathon runner in BBC interview.

- "I am selling fish (being selfish) for the game against Latvia at Hampden on Saturday." Craig Brown, Scottish manager.

- Credit card frauds are rising from 97 million in 1996 to over 700 Nelson Mandella this year.

- Despite universal condemnation round the world, the professor is going ahead with human genetic rnginrting

- Practise for Scottish Claymores at 8 am in the morning if Florida. Caption to photograph.

- "The future career of every Scottish child starts with a teacher." Scottish Executive TV advert.

- One of the principle tasks for the Irish Taoiseach is to open the memorial to the victims of famine in Ireland.

Answers

Margaret was a good queen and gave her clock to a beggar when she was out riding

Exercise A
Test your knowledge

The answers are given briefly below, but are fully dealt with in other lessons.

1. Should be *its*. It's stands for *it is*.
2. *During* and *in the course of* mean the same. Leave one out. The sentence would lose nothing by leaving out, *the whole of*.
3. *Unique* means only one exists, like the Taj Mahal. Use something like *unusual*.
4. How could the shopkeeper leave the bloody footsteps. The relative pronoun *who* must follow *killer*. Try rewriting the sentence with *who* coming after *killer*.
5. *and return to the given address* should come after *form*.
6. *May* not *can* and *your* in place of *you're*.
7. Correct. The verb *was* is right.
8. Correct. *Razed* does not need *to the ground*.
9. *Through the instrumentality of* is pompous, that is too fancy and high brow. *line* not Line
10. Omit *literally*.
11. The third line should have *anything*, not *nothing*.
12. Not luxuriant but *luxurious*. Luxuriant is used for growth like hair, a forest or grass.
13. Richard Branson is male and singular and *their* is plural. Put *his* eyes.
14. Leave out *final*.
15. *etc, etc* is to be scrubbed.
16. More wrong spelling. Put in *principle* and *separate*.

17. Weak sentence construction. After *field* omit *and men were working in it,* and put *and the men working there ran to help him.* One conjunction instead of two.
18. How can a tunnel be bottomless?
19. Escalate means to increase in volume or intensity, so *further* is not needed.
20. (a) General Custer carefully studied the surrounding territory *and* immediately ordered the attack on the Indians.

    (b) General Custer who had carefully studied the surrounding territory, immediately ordered the attack on the Indians.

    (c) Having carefully studied the map of the surrounding territory, General Custer immediately ordered the attack on the Indians.

    (a) Uses the conjunction *and*,(b) uses the relative pronoun *who*, and (c) the participle phrase, *having carefully studied......territory*.

Exercise 1.1
Your first homework

1. (a) "Will you walk into my parlour?" said the spider to the fly.
   (b) *The spider asked the fly if he would walk into his parlour.*
2. (a) "Stop the bus," yelled Margie, "i've left my handbag." (You could have an exclamation mark after *bag.*)
   (b) *Margie yelled at the bus to stop for she had left her handbag.*
3. (a) "It is easier to learn Bulgarian than I thought." claimed the young Greek girl.
   (b) *The young Greek girl claimed it was easier to learn Bulgarian than she had thought.*
4. (a) "Boil my eggs for three minutes," insisted Aunt Emma, "I like to dip my toast in the soft yolk."
   (b) *Aunt Emma insisted that her eggs were boiled for only three minutes as she liked to dip her toast into the soft yolk.*
5. (a) "If you are not up yet, Andy", mother shouted, you will be too late for your train." "Be down in a minute for my cornflakes," he shouted back.
   (b) *Mother shouted to Andy that if he wasn't up, he would miss his train. He shouted back he would be down in a minute for his cornflakes.* (You could leave out the full stop after train and put in *and he.*)
6. (a) "What can I get you for Christmas, my darling Clementine?" "One of those donut machines, so that I can make lips-smacking donuts in my very own kitchen."

(b) *Duncan asked Clementine what she would like for Christmas and she said one of those donut machines so she could make the donuts in her very own kitchen.*

7. (a) "Ladies and gentlemen," announced Miss Stirrat, "let me introduce our speaker for this evening. She is none other than the first woman to cross the Firth of Clyde in a bath tub from Brodick to Saltcoats. Miss le Farge, ladies and gentlemen!"

    (b) *Miss Stirrat introduced the speaker for the evening, who was none other than Miss le Farge, the first woman to cross the Firth of Clyde in a bath tub from Brodick to Saltcoats.*

8. (a) "What became of Ethan Frome and Ottokar Kraus?" my great uncle Tobias asked me. "I never heard of them," I replied, "but I'll do my best to find out."

    (b) *My great uncle Tobias asked me what had happened to Ethan Frome and Ottokar Kraus. I told him I'd never heard of them but I'd do my best to find out.*

9. (a) "Why," asked my pal, Geordie, "do TV adverts not give you a chance to jot down phone and e-mail numbers? It's as bad as the traffic lights that give you six and a half seconds, not enough time."

    (b) *My pal Geordie asked why TV adverts did not give you the chance to jot down phone and e-mail numbers. It was the same at traffic lights, six and a half seconds, not enough time.*

Exercise 2.1

Which of these is impossible?

All are possible!

- *My aunt's house.* Aunt Sara lives alone in her own house
- *My aunts' house.* Aunt Sara and Aunt Louisa, being sisters, live in the same house.
- *My aunt's houses.* Aunt Sara owns several houses, lives in one and lets the rest.
- *My aunts' houses.* Both aunts own houses, live together and rent the others.

Exercise 3.1
Make any necessary corrections

1. No correction It's equals it is.
2. *clinic's* is correct, being the short for 'clinic is'. No apostrophe for *citizens,* which is a simple plural.
3. You're right wherever you put the apostrophe for there could be one or more inspector.
4. *Children's tights.* You can never have childrens', remember? Also children's coats.
5. Winter's is singular, so an apostrophe is needed before the 's'.
6. Alter's is doubly wrong here. Again, no apostrophe for a simple plural, and only in churches are there altars.
7. The team's name is Hotspur, so apostrophe before the 's', and *goalkeeper's* is correct.
8. Even that stinker Stinko can take over only the supply of one world, thus *world's*.
9. "I've left my good umbrella in the ladies' cloakroom", the plural being *ladies*.
10. All correct. Repeat, never, never mens' or seamens'.

Exercise 4.1
Try these for yourself

1. Mr Winterton himself should have been made redundant for this two prong attack on his fellow Tory! Crass ineptitude is bad enough without the

blatant incompetence.
2. The first born in a family could hardly help the younger ones coming after them!
3. *terribly visually* is a waste of words.
4. What other kind of lunatics are there but crazy?
5. Congratulations to Mr Chapman for starting his speech at the beginning.
6. The commentator could simply have said, "Things are going from bad to worse at West Ham."
7. If you go back to the Middle Ages, you have to cover those hundreds of years.
8. You could leave out *The original prototype of*.
9. Simply omit *yet*. Or *still*.
10. It's always a *first priority* with politicians. *His priority* would be enough.

Exercise 6.1
For you to decipher

1. "...which belonged to Liz Taylor," refers to the £40,000 ring and not to her wedding finger. The phrase must come immediately after "wedding ring."
2. Simple. Replace 'the owner' with 'the seller'.
3. Put the phrase 'Three years after he died' at the start of the sentence.
4. Of course, we know a candle cannot shout for help. The phrase "when the candle blew out" may come at the start or the end of the sentence. My

preference is for the start, as it was the first of the three events:

"When the wind blew out the candle, they were frightened and shouted for help."

5. The drunk could have been fined for assaulting the plane, but it was more likely for thumping a passenger or crew member.

6. Were the councillors holding a conference about the esplanade or on the esplanade? Probably the former, but with councillors you never can tell!

7. When I read this many years ago, I pictured a WWI German pointed helmet, and worried about Fred sitting on such a helmet to write his first poem. I soon realised that his poem was *about* the helmet!

8. Can you decide who is standing at the street corner, the football scout or potential Michael Owens?

9. Michael did not get ten years for fraud at a US work camp, but for selling phony stocks and shares on Wall Street. The sentence must be rewritten:

"Convicted of fraud, fallen junk bond king, Michael Milken, is serving a ten year sentence at a US government work camp near San Franscisco."

10. If you are not a football fan you would not immediately realise it was Barrow Football Club that was fined, not a common wheelbarrow, a neolithic burial mound or a castrated pig.

Exercise 7.1
Correct the following

1. Mr Lawrence can build a home for you and himself but not for *I*. It must be the objective pronoun *me* after the preposition *for*.
2. Correct. He is older than I (am).
3. *We* is nominative (as is the subject of any sentence). Therefore, for *us* human beings. Objective *us* after *for*.
4. The subject of this sentence is *amount* singular and it must take a single predicate, *has* and not *have*. The amount of beer and whisky has plummeted.
5. Ian Wright, singular, and he has a singular predicate throughout the sentence. He *is* leaving football to take *his* talent into show business.
6. It is only a combination (of these methods) which *is* successful.
7. Us is an objective pronoun. How can us give the young a tip? Should be nominative, we.

Exercise 8.1
Parse the following

1. *I, p*ersonal pronoun, first person, singular, common gender (we don't know if *I* is masculine or feminine), nominative case, subject to the verb *promised*.

   Barbie, adjective, qualifying the noun *doll*. (The word *qualifying* means I'm not buying her any old doll, but a special one.)

   Birthday, noun, common, singular, common gender, objective after preposition, *for*. You might argue that *birthday* is an abstract noun as you cannot *see* it and that it is neuter.

2. Garden, adjective, describing the noun *gate*. *Weeded*, verb, past tense, active voice, predicate of *I*. *Garden*, noun, common, singular, neuter, objective case after the transitive verb, *weeded*.

3. *You*, personal pronoun, second person, common gender, nominative to verb, *need*.
   Balance, noun, singular, abstract, objective after the transitive verb, *need*. *Successfully*, adverb, positive degree, modifying verb, *walk*.

4. *Our*, possessive adjective, plural, describing MP. *And*, conjunction joining adjectives, *newest* and *youngest*. *Youngest*, adjective, *superlative degree*, qualifying *MP*.

Exercise 12.1
Using conjunctions

1. The Pilgrim Fathers **whose** ship was called the Mayflower, set sail for America in 1620.
2. The great storm, **which** raged two whole days, destroyed thousands of trees all over the land.
3. Joan of Arc, **who** was born in the tiny village of Domremy, led a French army against the English at the siege of Orleans.
4. Mozart wrote *The Magic Flute*, which is my favourite of all operas.
5. Mozart, **who** died when he was only 36, also composed *Figaro*.
6. My Grandad, **whose** luck is fantastic, won three prizes at the Bingo last night.
7. That storm, **that** papers hardly mentioned, kept me awake all night.
8. In his attic Curly has a big telescope, through **which** he studies the stars each night.
9. Al Jolson, **who** was born Asa Yoelson in Russia, became a famous singer and film star in the United States, **and** appeared in the first all talking picture, *The Jazz Singer,* in 1927.
10. When I heard an actor say, "Did they saw their way through?" I thought at first it was bad grammar, **but** seconds later I realised he was a detective investigating a burglary.

Exercise 13.1
Completing Sentences

1. Gasping for breath, the Kanaka pearl diver claimed he had been stung by a colonial coelenterate. "A what?" shouted his pal. "A colonial coelenterate, y'know, a Portuguese man of war."

2. Having no money in her purse, Queen Victoria was not at all amused when at the fair when her equerry could not produce a bob at the coconut shy.

3. Not knowing the risks of dealings on the Internet, Maddie and Mick Dobbs from Polperro booked a holiday in London and landed in London... Ontario.

4. Having reached the oasis, the two Foreign Legion deserters begged to be made blood brothers of the Bedouin, for they loved camel milk and would become camel minders.

5. Without having had her breakfast, Betty Boop got an earlier bus to town and headed for Koe's Eats and tucked into oranage juice, egg, bacon, black pudding, two sausages, tomato, fried bread, tea, toast and marmalade, which would keep her going till lunch time.

Exercise 13.2
Sentence Structure

1. "Soapy was in a bad mood because someone had turned on a Bunsen burner before leaving the science room." Using the conjunction *because* is probably the best way of joining.
2. "Smartypants Yogi Bear dearly loved *pickinic* baskets' which he sneaked out of tourists' cars but the park ranger nearly always caught him and he had to hand the baskets and apologise." You might have "Smarty pants Yogi Bear who loved pickinick baskets sneaked............ with the two conjunctions *but* then *and*.
3. "Michelangelo was a poet, painter, sculptor, architect and engineer whom many historians consider to be the cleverest man ever."
   Note again, the commas between topics in a list, except for the last two. Also using the objective pronoun whom in place of the objective pronoun him.
4. Minnehaha O'Toole was a Wishaw washerwoman whose daughter once climbed every greasy pole in the state of Wisconsin.
5. In Dumfriesshire near the Bellybought Hill is the little village with the littlest name, Ae which the BBC *Dictionary of Pronunciation* declares rhymes with *day*.
6. "This film is about a gigantic Caribbean octopus with 19 meter long tentacles that crunch every wooden ship carrying slaves bound for the underwater kingdom of Atlantica." **or** "This film,

about a gigantic Caribbean octopus with 19 meter tentacles, crunches ..."
7. "Alexandre Gustave Eiffel, a French engineer, designed the famous tower for the Paris Exhibition of 1898 and it was for many years, the highest man made structure in the world." A chance here to use a phrase in apposition, a *French engineer.*
8. The undercover police moved into the open air Saturday market where they arrested three members of a cigarette gang, one of whom escaped by punching a policeman. You could start with a present participle phrase, "Moving into the Saturday open market,, the undercover police ..."
9. "Aunt Jemima who is 87 years old does not look her age and her favourite pastime is crotcheting napkins and doyleys that she gives to relatives and friends at Christmas." Or You can start with "Not looking anything like her 87 years, Aunt Jemima's hobby is crotcheting napkins and doyleys that ..."
10. Sodium, a very corrosive metal and chlorine a most poisonous gas, unite to give sodium chloride, the very substance we call salt. The first two independent, simple sentences made into one with predicate, unite.
11. The world, being tipped at an angle of 23 1/2 degrees, gives us the Tropics of Cancer and Capricorn and in Britain, unequal day and night and the seasons.

12. "On being told that a 40 foot dragon was terrorising a village, Prince Aloysius grabbed his bum bag, fearlessly confronted the beast and knowing dragons love porridge, threw it lumps of cold porridge laced with sassafras oil which rendered it as docile as Larry The Lamb." A bit of juggling needed with four sentences and turning three into phrases like, *On being told* and *he knew* into *knowing*.

Exercise 14.1
Active to Passive

- Our tent was blown down by the wind and our sandwiches scoffed by a whippet.
- The Channel was flown by Louis Bleriot in 1909 and the Atlantic by Lindbergh in 1927.
- Ginty's window was not broken by our wee Benny.
- We were offered free tickets by Partick Thistle for Wednesday's big game.
- The winning goal in the World Cup final was snatched by Big Andy Gump.

Exercise 17.1
Word Strength

Arranging words in order of strength is a matter of opinion, so if my list does not agree with yours, do not be dismayed.

1. Infinitesimal, microscopic, minute, small.
2. Big, large, vast, colossal.
3. Annoyed, irritated, furious, livid.
4. Rigorous, stringent, harsh, brutal.
5. Lean, skinny, shrunken, skelletal.
6. Trot, sprint, hasten, bolt.
7. Imp, scallywag, rascal, villain.
8. Droll, funny, hilarious, side-splitting.
9. Satisfied, pleased, delighted, ecstatic.
10. Glum, sad, dejected, melancholic.